Facilitating Children's Learning in the EYFS

Facilitating Children's Learning in the EYFS

Ann Langston

 Open University Press

Open University Press
McGraw-Hill Education
McGraw-Hill House
Shoppenhangers Road
Maidenhead
Berkshire
England
SL6 2QL

email: enquiries@openup.co.uk
world wide web: www.openup.co.uk

and Two Penn Plaza, New York, NY 10121-2289, USA

First published 2014

A catalogue record of this book is available from the British Library

ISBN-13: 978-0-33-524761-5 (pb)
ISBN-10: 0-33-524761-X (pb)
eISBN: 978-0-33-524762-2

Library of Congress Cataloging-in-Publication Data
CIP data applied for

Typesetting and e-book compilations by
RefineCatch Limited, Bungay, Suffolk

Praise for this book

Contents

Figures

Tables

Introduction

This book is the first in a series centred on teaching and learning in the revised Statutory Early Years Foundation Stage (EYFS) framework (2012). It offers a broad exploration of the changes in the EYFS and how the EYFS framework creates both a context for learning and the basis of a curriculum for children from birth to five in early years settings in England. In doing so it sets out to identify some of the inherent tensions created by changes, beginning in Chapter 1 by examining whether the Revised EYFS remains a Principled Framework; turning, in Chapter 2, to consider what school readiness means for children, families and society and its implications for teaching and learning in the EYFS. Chapter 3 then explores why an understanding of child development is important for teaching and learning in the EYFS, whilst Chapter 4 focuses on the requirements relating to engaging parents in their children's learning throughout this phase. Chapter 5 explores how the type of pedagogy which contributes to children's care as well as their education has evolved in England and examines how integrating these distinct but complementary aspects can lead to successful learning and development. Proposing a definition for pedagogy in the EYFS, the chapter focuses on ways to develop teaching and learning which meets children's needs for security and safety alongside their desires for challenge and stimulation.

In Chapter 6, pedagogy in the Prime areas is explored, focusing on children from birth to three years of age; the same areas are then discussed in respect of children from three to six years of age in Chapter 7. Turning finally, in Chapters 8–11 to discussion of the Specific Areas of learning: Literacy, Mathematics, Understanding the World and Expressive Arts and Design the book concludes, in Chapter 12 with a consideration of some of the challenges practitioners and policy makers face as they consider the skills and knowledge today's young children will need by the year 2020 when they are young adults. Concluding that the future will be shaped by early education in the present, this chapter calls for a new debate about the direction of early childhood education in England, notwithstanding the recent review of the EYFS – since by omitting, Understanding the World and Expressive Arts and Design from a measure of a 'good level of development' in the EYFS these areas are effectively relegated to the second division, albeit that the EYFS suggests 'all areas are considered to be equally important'. As science is beginning to reveal, in a world which is rapidly changing, it may be that areas of learning such as Understanding the World and Expressive Arts and Design, which lead to creativity and connectedness, may be our touchstones for the future when consideration of others and inventiveness may be recognised as every bit as important as skills and attributes which are more highly valued currently.

1 The revised EYFS: A principled framework?

The revised Early Years Foundation Stage Framework (DfE, 2012), together with its accompanying principles, learning requirements and intended outcomes creates both a context for learning and the basis of a curriculum for children from birth to five in early years settings in England. The revised statutory document asserts that four guiding principles should shape practice in early years settings, explaining these in relation to the following dimensions: the uniqueness of the child; the importance of positive relationships in supporting children to be strong and independent; the significance of the environment including partnership between parents and carers and a recognition that children develop and learn in different ways, and it concludes that the framework is intended to be inclusive of all children.

However the statutory document offers few clues as to how the principles of the EYFS can be put into practice; though an accompanying document: *Development Matters* (DfE/EE, 2012) attempts to do so. The latter offers suggestions about observing a child's development to find out how a child is learning across age-related bands together with suggestions about what practitioners in an enabling environment might do or provide to support children's learning. Whilst the information contained within *Development Matters* is helpful it is not sufficient since it does not provide an in-depth rationale or frame of reference for understanding the EYFS. The absence of this discussion risks weakening the principles of the EYFS because whilst they are briefly referred to in both documents their significance appears diminished.

The inclusion of this chapter is intended to redress the balance so that the principles on which the EYFS (DfES, 2007) was based and on which the revised EYFS (DfE, 2012) claims to be based can be reviewed in the light of current developments and the information provided in the documents discussed. The sparsity of information in these documents is of particular concern for those entering the early years profession as well as for more experienced practitioners, many of whom contributed to debates about which principles should underpin the EYFS framework; the latter frequently expressing their concerns about which elements of the previous document remain valid. Without any written guidance one must assume that the Principles into Practice cards which accompanied the earlier version, remain useful though they are no longer part of the framework. This is regrettable, since whilst they were never statutory they did explain and exemplify how the EYFS principles could be put into practice. At the same time, *Development Matters*, also a non-statutory document, re-presents the practice underpinning each principle. So how does it and the revised statutory EYFS now explain the principles to which the latter devotes fewer than one hundred words?

A Unique Child

In the revised EYFS the principle: A Unique Child is: '*Every child is a **unique child**, who is constantly learning and can be resilient, capable, confident and self-assured*' (DfE, 2012: 3). Whilst the same principle in the earlier EYFS (2007) stated: '*Every child is a competent learner from birth who can be resilient, capable, confident and self-assured*' (DfES, 2007: 9). The differences between the two are almost undetectable and mainly semantic – the changed wording intended to simplify and make the document more accessible. But what has been lost is the child being viewed as a *competent learner from birth* – this notion was derived from a body of research which underpinned an influential document focused on the education of children from birth to three years of age in England: *Birth to Three Matters* (DfES, 2003: 5). However, importantly, what has been retained is the view of every child as unique and different from every other child. This implies that in the EYFS every child has the capacity to learn and that their experiences should be personalised. The way this can be achieved is implied rather than explicit although it is stated in the revised document: '*Practitioners must consider the individual needs, interests, and stage of development of each child in their care, and must use this information to plan a challenging and enjoyable experience for each child in all of the areas of learning and development*' (DfE, 2012: 6).

Putting the Unique Child principle into practice

In order to put the Unique Child principle into practice the revised EYFS identifies that experiences provided for children should be both challenging and enjoyable and based around their:

- Needs
- Interests
- Stage(s) of development

In the earlier EYFS (2007) several of these areas were partially explained in the commitments to this principle:

- **Child Development** *'babies and children develop in individual ways and at varying rates. Every area of development – physical, cognitive, linguistic, spiritual, social and emotional is equally important'*.
- **Inclusive Practice** *'the diversity of individuals and communities is valued and respected. No child or family is discriminated against'*.
- **Keeping Safe** *'Young children are vulnerable. They develop resilience when their physical and psychological well-being is protected by adults'*.
- **Health and Well-Being** *'Children's health is an integral part of their emotional, mental, social, environmental and spiritual well-being and is supported by attention to these aspects'* (DfES, 2007).

These commitments highlight the ways in which children are unique; they also underscore the interconnection between physical and mental health, well-being and development, together with the significance of the role adults play in ensuring that diversity is valued and that children are kept safe from harm by adults who care for their physical and psychological well-being. Much of this is implicit in the revised framework, however *Development Matters* also provides further guidance about what practitioners should do in order to support the child; this suggests that in order to put this principle into practice practitioners should:

- *'understand and observe each child's development and learning, assess progress, plan for next steps*
- *support babies and children to develop a positive sense of their own identity and culture*
- *identify any need for additional support*
- *keep children safe*
- *value and respect all children and families equally'* (DfE/EE, 2012: 2).

What is suggested addresses most of the commitments; in order to put the unique child principle into practice it may be helpful for leaders, managers and practitioners to consider the questions in Table 1.1 and their own responses before reviewing the accompanying responses. These responses are not offered as solutions; they are possibilities to consider in the light of discussion of the questions. The purpose of this exercise is to review the way the setting puts into practice the principle: A Unique Child.

Further questions, not addressed here, relate to who will help the practitioner to identify and meet the needs of each unique child in their care, together with considerations of whether particular resources will be required

Table 1.1 The Unique Child exercise

Question	Your Response	Response
What do I know about this child?		• The child is a person first, then a family member who is part of a community. Understanding this helps us to begin to plan for this unique child whose personality, temperament, physical and mental health and experiences are different from every other child we may encounter.
What does this child need?		• This area has many connections with children's rights and determining the meaning of 'needs' deserves further investigation beyond this book since without a definition there is little clarity about its meaning in the EYFS. • If we take the 'needs' to be universal then the following are givens in psychological terms: the need for love and security; the need for new experiences; the need for praise and recognition; the need for responsibility (Pringle, 1980). • Whilst the basic physical and safety needs described by Maslow (1987) include: protection from dangerous or threatening events and having access to food, water, warmth, shelter and clothing. • At the same time individual children also need different things at different times such as the need for reassurance and the need to be supported through difficult life events. • All children, should be treated with respect, compassion and understanding.

How can I best support this child to develop and learn in this setting?		• The way practitioners can support each unique child best is by getting to know them well through engaging with them and their parents, and, if necessary, practitioners at previous settings and/or other professionals that have supported the child. • This knowledge of the child leads to an understanding of the child's interests and their present capabilities. The way we further this understanding of children is through building relationships with them – by talking to them and playing alongside them, looking out for what they enjoy doing and who they enjoy being with and through discussing their development with them, their parents and other practitioners in the setting. • The picture of the child which is created from all of this interaction and observation is the starting point for supporting the child's future development and learning. • From here practitioners may wish to familiarise themselves with the broad age bands in *Development Matters* and to consider what the next steps might be for each child in all of the areas of learning.

to make this happen, as well as how and when practitioners will evaluate the effectiveness of the approach taken.

Positive Relationships

The principle, Positive Relationships, is defined in the revised EYFS as: *'Children learn to be strong and independent through positive relationships'*

(DfE, 2012: 3). Again it is evident that in the interests of accessibility this principle has been abbreviated and the qualifying phrase '*from a base of loving and secure relationships with parents and/or a key person*' (DfES, 2007: 9) has been placed elsewhere. However, whilst explicit reference to this has been lost in the principle itself, very positively the significance of the key person role has been retained, found in a short paragraph, stating: '*Each child must be assigned a key person*' (DfE, 2012: 7). The EYFS (2007) commitments linked to this principle are:

- 'Respecting each other – *Every interaction is based on caring professional relationships and respectful acknowledgement of the feelings of children and their families.*
- Parents as Partners – *Parents are children's first and most enduring educators. When parents and professionals work together in early years settings, the results have a positive impact on children's development and learning.*
- Supporting learning – *Warm, trusting, relationships with knowledge-able adults support children's learning more effectively than any amount of resources.*
- Key Person – *A key person has special responsibilities for working with a small number of children, giving them the reassurance to feel safe and cared for and building relationships with parents*' (DfES, 2007).

This is in addition to the explanation of practice in *Development Matters* describing positive relationships as:

- '*warm and loving, and foster*(ing) *a sense of belonging*
- *sensitive and responsive to the child's needs, feelings and interests*
- *supportive of the child's own efforts and independence*
- *consistent in setting clear boundaries*
- *stimulating*
- *built on key person relationships in early years settings*' (DfE/EE, 2012: 2).

Putting the Positive Relationships principle into practice

In practical terms what does this principle require practitioners to consider in order to develop positive relationships? Again it is important to reflect on some pertinent questions in Table 1.2, and once again consider some responses which may support discussions as practitioners focus on the principle and develop ownership of it in relation to their own setting:

Table 1.2 The Positive Relationships exercise

Question	Your Response	Response
What does the principle look like in practice?		• This principle is focused on professional interactions which are sensitive to the feelings of children and their families. • *Development Matters* synthesises this in terms of relationships being sensitive and responsive yet warm and loving, setting boundaries for children's behaviour and based on the key person relationship. • Practically speaking positive relationships are based on mutual respect, with all those involved accepting and valuing the contributions of the other people, including children. • In the EYFS relationships extend to the interactions of caregivers with the child, between children and with one another as well as other people within and beyond the setting. • Promoting this principle effectively will require recognition by leaders of the importance of making connections with parents, children, community members and other professionals and listening to their opinions, valuing their contributions and engaging in continuing dialogue with them.

(*Continued*)

Table 1.2 *(Continued)*

Question	Your Response	Response
What is the role of the key person in promoting positive relationships?		• According to the revised document the key person's role in relationships is to *'offer a settled relationship for the child and build a relationship with their parents'* (DfE, 2012: 18). • The description in the EYFS statutory document does not fully describe the importance of attachment and the key person's role in this respect. • The key person is highly important in helping the child to cope with separation from their primary caregiver, and helping the child to negotiate and develop relationships with other children and with other members of staff.
How does the setting support the key person through appropriate supervision?		• The statutory document states: *'Effective supervision provides support, coaching and training for the practitioner and promotes the interests of children'* with opportunities provided for staff to *'discuss any issues – particularly concerning children's development or well-being'* (ibid.: 17). • Supervision practice will vary from setting to setting; however, leaders and managers should provide regular support for practitioners in their key person role. • Appropriate supervision would include discussions of how the child has settled into the setting; how the child has been supported to separate from the main carer; how the child has been supported to get to know other children and other practitioners, and the impact of the emotional demands of their role on the key person – especially those who work with vulnerable children.

The questions that remain relate to who will help the practitioner to meet the needs of each unique child in their key person group, together with considerations of whether particular strategies will be required to support the child further (this might include re-assigning the child to a key person they, rather than adults, have selected) and how a key person is to be given the support they need (particularly when aspects of their role become challenging).

Enabling Environments

The principle Enabling Environments which in the revised EYFS is explained as: '*Children learn and develop well in **enabling environments**, in which their experiences respond to their individual needs and there is a strong partnership between practitioners and parents and/or carers*' (ibid.: 3). This is expressed in the commitments relating to this principle in EYFS (2007):

- Observation, Assessment and Planning – '*Babies and young children are individuals first, each with a unique profile of abilities. Schedules and routines should flow with the child's needs. All planning starts with observing children in order to understand and consider their current interests, development and learning.*
- Supporting Every Child – *The environment supports every child's learning through planned experiences and activities that are challenging but achievable.*
- The Learning Environment – *A rich and varied environment supports children's learning and development. It gives them the confidence to explore and learn in secure and safe, yet challenging indoor and outdoor spaces.*
- The Wider Context – *Working in partnership with other settings, other professionals and with individuals and groups in the community supports children's development and progress towards . . . being healthy, staying safe, enjoying and achieving, making a positive contribution and economic well-being*' (DfES, 2007).

There is some symmetry between what is described in the two frameworks though again there is little detail in the revised EYFS. However, *Development Matters* suggests that enabling environments do the following:

- *Value all people*
- *Value learning*

And offer:

- *'stimulating resources, relevant to all the children's cultures and communities*
- *rich learning opportunities through play and playful teaching*
- *support for children to take risks and explore'* (DfE/EE, 2012: 2).

There is little to disagree with here though the important role adults play in creating an emotionally safe environment, and their importance in supporting children emotionally is understated. It is widely accepted that in early years settings, adults, above all else, are the most important and beneficial resource for young children. Review in Table 1.3 the questions this raises about how this principle can be put into practice:

Table 1.3 The Enabling Environments exercise

Question	Your Response	Response
What is an enabling environment for young children in out of home settings?		• This varies according to children's individual stages of development and, whilst some aspects of the physical space may remain the same, interactions and resources often alter according to children's interests, the seasons, weather or different events. • An enabling environment is not limited to physical features such as resources; it also relates to spaces in and out of doors and to the emotional 'space' – the 'climate' created by the feelings of all those who are in it, including the children. This will be culturally sensitive and will value all children and families equally. • More importantly an enabling environment is one in which the child feels comfortable and competent; and confident both in themselves and others. • An enabling environment is one in which the child is able to be themselves, knowing that they are accepted for who they are, rather than for what they know or can do; where their talents can grow and their interests are nurtured.

How is an enabling environment created?		• An enabling environment is created when leaders and managers, together with practitioners, parents and other partners, consider what is important in order for children to achieve maximum benefit from their experiences. • This means that rules for self-care and caring and kindness towards others are developed with children, alongside rules for keeping safe (where risks are assessed and managed) and approaches to teaching and learning are identified. • When these dimensions are addressed learning develops from children's interests.
How does an enabling environment evolve and change?		• An enabling environment evolves in relation to the children's development – resources may change to accommodate either a new phase of development for particular children or in response to new interests. • Children may become extremely interested in following particular lines of enquiry – perhaps related to an interest in 'parties' – when learning may begin indoors with the creation of party foods and invitations but then may begin to follow different directions – creating 'shows', for example. This will often mean that resources have to be added and enhancements provided to support play. • Similarly as children mature and develop they are likely to prefer some resources more than others and be given access to resources that would not be suitable for younger children, such as sewing materials or small objects such as buttons.

Other questions that frequently arise relating to this principle focus on how the curriculum can be supported both in and out of doors and whether what is on offer inside should be reflected outside, or offer radically different experiences. A further issue to consider related to outdoor provision is whether and to what extent learning can take place out of doors in all types of weather – the key concerns here are with risk assessment and the availability of appropriate clothing for children and practitioners.

Learning and Development

The final principle, Learning and Development, is explained in the revised EYFS as: *'Children develop and learn in different ways and at different rates'* (DfE, 2012: 3). This is identical to the original principle which also had the additional words: *'and all areas of learning and development are equally important and inter-connected'*. The relevant commitments in the EYFS (2007) are:

- Play and Exploration – *'Children's play reflects their wide ranging and varied interests and preoccupations. In their play children learn at their highest level. Play with peers is important for children's development.*
- Active Learning – *Children learn best through physical and mental challenges. Active learning involves other people, objects, ideas and events that engage and involve children for sustained periods.*
- Creativity and Critical Thinking – *When children have opportunities to play with ideas in different situations and with a variety of resources, they discover connections and come to new and better understandings and ways of doing things. Adult support in this process enhances their ability to think critically and ask questions'* (DfES, 2007).

The three commitments are readily identifiable as the 'characteristics of effective learning' referred to in both the revised EYFS and in *Development Matters*. These have now been simplified and reduced to phrases which are like shortcuts to the commitments, but because they have become separated from them risk losing their power. 'Play and Exploration' is described as *'engagement'* with the features of this important area described as: *'Finding out and exploring; playing with what they know; being willing to "have a go"'* (DfE/EE, 2012: 5). Whilst this does emphasise the importance of play and exploration, the richness and reality of what it is to play in early childhood settings is not explored in any depth and might be the focus of discussion in settings.

The distinguishing feature of 'Active learning' is defined as *'motivation'* which involves *'being involved and concentrating; keeping* [sic] *trying; enjoying achieving what they set out to do'* (ibid.: 5). The third characteristic:

'Creating and Thinking Critically', described as *'thinking'*, refers to children *'having their own ideas; making links; choosing ways to do things'* (ibid.: 5). Clearly many positive messages have been retained in relation to these commitments which form part of this principle – however this is also an area of extensive change.

Areas of Learning and Development

The significant and major change between the two EYFS frameworks (2007, 2012) is in relation to the Areas of Learning and Development. In the EYFS (2007) there were six areas; in the revised version seven areas and the latter confirms that *'All areas of learning and development are important and inter-connected'* (DfE, 2012: 4). This is significant since the areas of learning have been separated into two groups – the Prime and Specific areas. This division is important for a number of reasons since, as will become clear, an initial focus on the Prime areas highlights the importance of childhood development in shaping children's lives and life chances. Comparing the two frameworks it is obvious that the main change is to Communication, Language and Literacy which has been subdivided into separate areas: a) Communication and Language and b) Literacy. Other changes are mainly organisational or semantic – the latter in the interests of plain English. The areas of learning in development now appear in the following two groups:

Prime Areas	Specific Areas
• Personal, Social and Emotional Development	• Literacy
• Communication and Language	• Mathematics
• Physical Development	• Understanding the World
	• Expressive Arts and Design

The revised EYFS describes the three prime areas as: *'particularly crucial for igniting children's curiosity and enthusiasm for learning, and for building their capacity to learn, form relationships and thrive'* (ibid.: 4). It indicates that it is through four *specific* areas, that *'the three prime areas are strengthened and applied'* (ibid.: 5). This appears to prioritise learning in the prime areas however at the same time it is indicated that practitioners should plan for *'challenging and enjoyable experience for each child in all of the areas of learning and development'* (ibid.: 6), whilst the emphasis for those working with the youngest children should be on the prime areas; the balance shifting towards *'a more equal focus on all areas of learning as children grow in confidence and ability within the three prime areas*' (ibid.: 6). The rationale for this division is indicative of increasing recognition of the importance of the prime areas for all other learning – particularly emotional development, which is seen as highly significant as repeated studies have revealed (National Research Council and Institute of Medicine (Shonkoff) 2000).

Putting the Learning and Development principle into practice

In order to put the Learning and Development principle into practice consider some of the following questions in Table 1.4 and your responses in order to come to a view of learning which fits the philosophy of the setting and maintains the spirit of the EYFS. Some of the following questions might inform thinking in this area:

Table 1.4 Learning and Development issues

Question	Your Response	Response
How can we strike the correct 'balance' between the Prime and Specific areas for the age/stage of children in different groups?		• Striking the right balance relies on practitioners having a good knowledge of each child and making a professional judgement about the next steps for their development and learning. • Groups of children will have different needs, some of which will be transient – a child who has a temporary condition, such as 'glue ear' affecting their speech and language will need more support in Communication and Language, whilst a child who is finding it difficult to settle into a setting will need more emotional support.

How are the characteristics of effective learning planned for and promoted in the setting?		• The EYFSP also addresses the characteristics of effective learning. The EYFS refers to 'how children learn' endorsing practice which is based on play, exploration, critical thinking and active learning – provided that teaching supports this appropriately. The term is not restricted to learning; it is also used with reference to teaching. • When planning starts with what children are interested in it follows that plans reflect the different ways that children learn.
Development Matters refers to *'playful teaching'*; what does this mean in my setting and what does it look like?		• This is a challenging question – playful teaching has come into common usage but in reality has never been discussed in relation to the EYFS so it will have different meaning for different people. • Having a discussion about playful teaching can be extremely challenging – what one person regards as 'playful' may be very different from another person's view.

There are still many questions left unanswered in terms of teaching and learning in the EYFS however much of the remainder of this book focuses on issues to instigate discussion, raise and answer some questions, as well as to provide provocation for further thought.

In conclusion, it should now be apparent that the four principles of the EYFS are a device for thinking about the relationship between the child, teaching, the environment and what is to be learned throughout the period of the EYFS: the most significant time in a young child's life for their physical, social and emotional development and for their communication and language development as well as for the beliefs and attitudes they form about themselves as people and learners.

The retention of the principles from one framework to the next is not in doubt – the lack of discussion about what they represent and how they can be developed in practice in the documentation is however, an issue. Nevertheless, this should not deter practitioners from using the principles as a lens to review and question their own practice. Used in this way the principles can act as a benchmark for what is appropriate practice in the early years whilst supporting professional discussions about young children's development, how they learn and what is effective practice in teaching the very youngest children. These dialogues are particularly significant because as indicated in a recent early years study: '*Encounters between people are fluid and never the same twice. For this reason it is important for all educators to be reflective practitioners, sensitive to children and knowledgeable about how they develop*' (McCain *et al.*, 2011: 54).

The following chapter focuses on the concept of school readiness – a contentious issue which should be understood in the context of global concerns which have led to recognition of the importance of early childhood education in the lives of young children.

2   School readiness

Having considered the principles of the EYFS (2007, 2012) this chapter now explores debates about the meaning of 'school readiness' as described in the revised EYFS (2012), together with the tensions that this creates for early childhood education, where the notion of instrumental education is frequently rejected in favour of arguments which focus on present benefits for children, as opposed to those which will influence their future learning and life chances. This is followed by an exploration of the interdependent dimensions of school readiness which rest with the family, school and community each of which provides a context for considerations of the child's development and expectations when they attend school.

In identifying a conceptual framework to understand school readiness a UNICEF paper argues that the simplicity of the term '*belies the complexity of the concept and its relevance for development*' (Britto, 2012: 4) suggesting that because of limited access to information in some parts of the world there are different interpretations of 'school readiness', some of which may have led to practices based on outdated models of education for young children. This is due in part to the fact that there is no 'one size fits all' definition and also to perceptions about what 'school' actually is, or means.

In England the legal age for a child starting school is the term after their fifth birthday but in reality since September 2011, the school starting date for the majority of children has been from the September following their fourth birthday. In effect this means that a child born on 31 August will attend school a year earlier than a child born on 1 September in the same year. When calculated in months the age difference between children in any one reception class in England could be as much as 11 months; as a proportion of the life of a four-year-old this is approximately 25% – which is why understanding children's development is extremely important if teaching and learning is to be appropriate for individual children. Hence recent concerns about reference in the revised Early Years Foundation Stage to teaching and learning which ensures '*children's "school readiness" and gives children the broad range of knowledge and skills that provide the right foundation for good future progress through school and life*' (DfE, 2012: 2).

A further confusion in this debate is that the only other reference in the revised EYFS to school readiness is in discussion of *'readiness for Year 1'*. A final concern is that since school readiness is neither discussed nor defined in the EYFS it remains open to individual interpretation which could risk the loss of children's entitlement to a play-based curriculum.

Beyond this country there have been international debates on the importance of school readiness, though it has been defined differently by different groups. In 2002 a United Nations statement described *'a world fit for children'* (UN, 2002: 2) in which all children get the best possible start in life, and have access to a quality basic education with ample opportunity to develop their individual capacities in a safe and supportive environment through the promotion of their physical, psychological, spiritual, social, emotional, cognitive and cultural development – as a matter of national and global priority. In itself this does not provide a definition, though it does set out the parameters of children's education across the domains which are readily recognised as the foundations of early childhood education in this and other countries.

The character of debates prior to and since this statement have been widespread, particularly in the United States, with different states taking a variety of approaches to influence young children's development, many of them adjusting in line with increasing findings from neuroscience. For example, in a technical report from the American Academy of Paediatrics focusing on school readiness there is discussion of the influence of the country's National Education Goals Panel which took as its first priority that all children would start school 'ready to learn'. Concerns about young children's readiness for learning have continued to emerge because of fears about an increasing reliance on the need for human, rather than physical or structural capital (Britto, 2012) because better educated citizens are seen as better contributors to a country's economy.

A major challenge in the concept of school readiness is that it appears to devalue early childhood education, apparently positioning it outside of 'school' education suggesting that it is a period of preparation for it. This is not helpful for a number of reasons. Firstly, whilst school readiness remains undefined, even though many would accept it is 'a good thing', it is open to misinterpretation. Secondly, a further dilemma is that it creates tensions between the belief that early education is beneficial for children, compared with the view that it is ultimately of greater benefit to society – clearly most challenging for those who believe young children have a right to high quality early education. The acid test of whether these positions can be reconciled relies on convincing doubters that intrinsic and extrinsic benefits are not mutually exclusive. This appears to have been achieved in many US states but in England this is not the case, suggesting that there should be more discussion of the concept if it is to be whole-heartedly adopted on this side of the Atlantic: a major concern being that a child considered not to be ready for school might be viewed as in some way deficit, the 'problem' apparently located within the child, rather than elsewhere.

A further issue is that since the EYFS framework relates to children up to the end of their reception year in primary schools, those attending reception classes and those taking up the free 15 hour offer of early education in a maintained nursery or nursery class, are technically school 'pupils'; this has the potential to create confusion. Efforts to clarify this followed a government consultation on the revised EYFS in 2011 which indicated: 'Around a third of respondents were concerned by the term "school readiness" which they believed compromised the assertion that the EYFS is an important phase in its own right rather than being preparation for school' (DfE, 2011: 31). It was also indicated that online feedback had suggested 'that the definition could be clearer, including to reflect that children join school in Reception class when the EYFS is the required curriculum'. In response to these concerns it was accepted that this had caused some anxieties: 'and that there may [have been] a concern about too strong a focus on formal education too soon' which the government considered was 'unwarranted because school readiness should be understood in a broad sense' (ibid.: 2), going on to explain that this broad view would include important elements such as children being able to 'walk and run, to talk and understand, and learn to relate to others, as well as beginning to read and write and use numbers' (ibid.: 2). Finally, it asserted: 'Readiness for Year 1 and later life depends on an approach to child development which combines play and teaching in safe environments in the early years and in which children experience warm positive interaction, and can explore and learn, with appropriate support from skilled adults. These are all important elements of "school readiness" that are reflected in the new Early Learning Goals (ELGs)' (ibid.: 2).

So, although the position is never stated unequivocally, what is apparent is that when young children in England attend reception and nursery classes they are considered to be pre-schoolers, indicating that school readiness refers to readiness for Year One of primary school. However this important message risks being lost because to be engaged in becoming ready for school when children attend school is something of an impossibility.

Turning the argument on its head to consider whether schools are ready for children is not a new idea, though most would argue that this should be in the wider context of the individual child, the family, the culture and the community and should include the induction of children as they make the transition from pre-school to school. A recent report indicated 'Elementary schools must be ready to "take the baton" to support young children and engage families. Just as children must be ready for school, **schools must be ready to** *promote the full range of early learning, including social, emotional and physical development. They must also be prepared for the growing diversity of our child population'* (CED, 2012: 20). Another report suggests that many factors could ensure schools' readiness for children including: *'Facilitating smooth transition between home and school, including cultural sensitivity'* whilst *'Striving for continuity between early care and education programmes and elementary school'* (High *et al.*, 2008: 2). The difficulty associated with this as a universal approach is that, as UNICEF noted, whilst pre-schools are different all over the world, they share a common characteristic which is that: *'Most early childhood care and education programmes differ greatly compared to the education philosophy, teaching style and structure of primary school'* (Britto, 2012: 11). In consideration of this finding it suggests that the greater the gap between the two systems (pre-schools and schools) the greater the challenge is likely to be for the children, citing transition as a major hurdle. However, on a very positive note, a major difference in this country is that of the 98% of three- and four-year-old children taking up their entitlement to 15 hours of free education in the EYFS, 27% attend nursery schools and nursery classes in primary schools and a further 32% attend infant (reception) classes in primary schools, the remainder attending private and voluntary provision or independent schools (DfE/SFR13, 2012). This suggests that, at the very least, for the 59% attending maintained schools, transition between educational phases could be more contiguous to ensure that children's experiences matched their needs appropriately

Ready for Year One of primary school

Arguments that the EYFS should be focused mainly on the social and emotional aspects of learning, whilst areas of learning such as literacy and numeracy are more appropriately developed in Year One of school appear attractive. However, what has now been established is that: *'Despite the polarisation that has existed between those who emphasise literacy and those who emphasise social-emotional development . . . Social-emotional development is the foundation for cognitive development. It's not either/or. Both social skills and literacy skills are needed to be successful in school and life'* (Rhode Island Kids Count, 2005: 55). This suggests that the emphasis on social-emotional development begun in the EYFS period should be maintained throughout the early years of schooling since supporting children in these areas is likely to be beneficial not only in relation to PSED but also in terms of their broader cognitive development.

What is a continuing concern subsequent to the EYFS is the 'how' and the 'what' of learning in Year One of children's primary school education, considering their ages and stages of development on entry to this phase of schooling. Just as the youngest child in a reception class will be eleven months younger than the oldest the difference is still stark in Year One. This means that these young children will be at very different stages developmentally from one another and whilst there are always exceptions to any rule the evidence from a number of studies shows: '*large and significant differences between August- and September-born children in terms of their cognitive skills, whether measured using national achievement tests or alternative indicators such as the British Ability Scales. These gaps were particularly pronounced when considering teacher reports of children's performance; moreover, they were also present when considering differences in socio-emotional development*' (Crawford et al., 2011: 2).

As one would expect, these differences dissipate over time, but in spite of this, research has shown that August born children go on to undertake vocational, as opposed to academic qualifications, more frequently than their older peers and fewer attend a Russell Group university at the end of sixth form. This serves as a point for leaders to pause when considering the 'how' of teaching in Year One since it is clear that there are developmental differences between the youngest and oldest children in any cohort, suggesting that provision should be differentiated accordingly. Matching provision in Year One to the needs of all children would also reduce the risks associated with the loss of learning momentum in transition between the phases, since children would settle more readily into an environment which shared features of high quality EYFS provision, incorporating the EYFS principles and related approaches to teaching and learning. This is stressed in the Early Years Foundation Stage Profile Handbook which states: '*The transition between the EYFS and Year 1 should be seamless. EYFS practitioners and Year 1 teachers should work together to ensure that children's learning experiences in the final year of the EYFS are valuable in themselves, and prepare the ground for their move to Year 1. It is important that Year 1 builds on the successful principles and approach encapsulated in the EYFS*' (STA, 2012: 13). However, unless and until corresponding guidance emerges through the revised National Curriculum in relation to practice in Year One this may remain a hope rather than an aspiration.

Beyond debates of the readiness of children for school and the readiness of schools for children lie those focusing on what society, particularly parents, want for children and what they need to do in order to support children to benefit from their time in school. Not unexpectedly almost all discussions of school readiness refer to the significant role of socio-economic factors in shaping children's chances of success in school, describing a combination of factors which have a powerful influence on young children's 'readiness' for school. Indeed, in a UK early years policy report reviewing the factors accounting for differences in outcomes between children from more and less advantaged backgrounds it was noted that '*factors such as parenting style and the home environment, maternal and child health care, early childhood care and education and maternal education and other demographic factors – together help explain why low income children come to schools less ready to learn, and why high income children come to school with an advantage'* (Waldfogel and Washbrook, 2008: 3). However a European report focused on tackling social and cultural inequalities through early childhood education indicates that *'low income . . . alone may not be a decisive factor'* rather it is often a *combination of factors* that leads to *'consequences for child development'* (EACEA, 2009: 19).

More recent UK research suggests that when parental education and parental income are factored in even children from middle income families fare worse than those from higher income families. This is explained by a gap in the vocabulary of middle income families who are understood to provide *'a less rich learning environment in the home'* (Washbrook and Waldfogel, 2011: 2) compared with that experienced by their better off peers. Similarly greater behaviour problems of children in this group are explained by the experiences of mothers with *'less good mental well-being'* (ibid.: 2) and greater social isolation.

An antidote offered by policy makers to these and other factors is a mixture of universal and targeted services provided through support for children and families in wide ranging strategies such as the Foundation Years website, which describes itself as providing *'information for all families in England with children under the age of 5'* and initiatives such as provision in children's centres, whose core purpose is: *'to improve outcomes for young children and their families, with a particular focus on the most disadvantaged, so children are equipped for life and ready for school, no matter what their background or family circumstances'* (DfE website). Many more initiatives focus on this area – all recognising the importance of cyclical patterns of

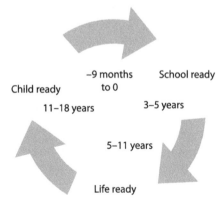

Figure 2.1 A Virtuous Circle. Graham Allen (2011) *Early Intervention: The next steps.* London: Cabinet Office

difficulty that lead into or spring from one another such as parenting, failed relationships, mental health problems and so on. The simplest representation of the 'solution' to the school readiness dilemma is set out in Figure 2.1 which was included in an independent report to the government on early intervention, showing that if parents are *'child ready'* then their children will become *'school ready'* who, eventually will grow into people who become *'child ready' parents'* (Allen, 2011: 8).

Concluding that whilst *'the great driving force for deciding the future of children is their parents'* an earlier report argued that *'the very best governments, communities and families can do is to support parents to enable them to be more effective agents of change for their children'* (Field, 2010: 18). The solution to this problem is neither straightforward nor within the focus of this publication, however it is worth considering what, as members of communities, schools and settings can do to support parents to ensure that their children benefit from their early educational experiences. There are no easy answers; however, there are both some quick wins and some long term strategies that derive from working in partnership with parents which will be discussed more fully in Chapter 4. One thing is clear many parents and teachers have differing perspectives about 'readiness' for school and two US studies (Ackerman and Barnet, 2005) found that whilst 58% of parents believed readiness was linked to things such as counting to twenty and beyond and knowing different letters, fewer than 10% of kindergarten teachers believed this was necessary. This suggests that effective communication between families and schools requires greater investment if both groups are to meet children's needs appropriately as learners.

A further issue is that there is neither consensus nor clarity about the term 'school readiness'. Seeking a definition might include rejecting the words whilst supporting the principle of helping parents and their children to gain maximum benefit from the offer of high quality pre-school education under the guidance of knowledgeable early childhood educators. If this were to happen alongside a public debate about school readiness it is possible that a definition could be agreed and a policy articulated that would be embraced by all those who influence children's lives including parents and policy makers as well as community members such as health professionals and educators.

Effective practice

The EYFS is intended amongst other things to promote *'school readiness'* (DfE, 2012: 2). In the EYFS the term 'school readiness' refers to preparation for Year One and it is important that it is understood in that context since otherwise each stage of education could be viewed as preparation for the next which would undermine the value of any particular stage. Clarifying what is meant by 'school readiness' will ensure that unrealistic expectations are not placed on children or on the pre-schools they attend. Indeed children are likely to be as 'ready' for school as schools are ready for them. Acknowledging this places the responsibility not on the child but upon parents, pre-schools and schools who, ideally, should work together to ensure children experience seamless transitions between settings whether they are at the start or at the end of the EYFS.

In any discussions of transition schools and settings should endeavour to work together and with parents to reduce discontinuities for the child so that they have the best possible start in terms of:

- Becoming familiar with the Key Person initially, then other significant adults in the setting
- Becoming familiar with the setting and how to find what they need and feel at home in it
- Developing new friends
- Understanding the rules and expectations for behaviour

If the EYFS (2012) principles are to be put into practice time should be set aside to ensure that positive relationships are developed between different settings and within and between schools since those who work with the same children are united in trying to achieve the same thing – positive outcomes for children. By working together in a principled way it may be possible to re-define 'school readiness' as something that is everybody's responsibility, rather than something that children are expected to work towards or become. Underpinning this approach will be recognition of the importance of child development in understanding children's very varied starting points, an area addressed in the following chapter.

3   The significance of child development in the revised EYFS

Why is child development important to teaching and learning in the EYFS?

This chapter sets out not to explain child development, since this has been done in depth elsewhere (Langston and Doherty, 2012: 17–32) but to explore some of the issues surrounding this area in the light of emerging debates in relation to the influence of findings from neuroscience on early education. It will also consider some important questions and challenges which practitioners, leaders and managers face and which they often raise in continuing professional development discussions. Teasing out these concerns further it emerges that increasing demands (real or perceived) made on staff, and different interpretations about what to prioritise in the EYFS creates tensions. Clearly, when this is the case, many things including the significance of early childhood development, can be overlooked – in order to counteract these concerns the following section focuses on the significance of child development to teaching and learning in the EYFS.

Child development is important to teaching and learning in the EYFS mainly because of the profound impact that early experiences have on children's attitudes and beliefs about themselves: first as people, and then as learners. At the same time, concerns expressed by influential economists across the globe, including university professors and bankers recognise the importance of child development to societies both socially and economically. Indeed at a recent conference speaking on behalf of an American bank, JP Morgan Chase, the Executive Director said: '*There is a rich body of evidence that . . . shows the correlation between high quality early learning and better life outcomes*' (Jasmin, 2012). From this it is clear that the early childhood education (ECE) is being viewed as a major player in setting children on a positive personal and educational trajectory (even though the reasons for this may not be consistent with what many early years educators believe to be important). As a result this area is coming under increasing scrutiny and the whole arena of ECE is now of interest to a variety of stakeholders. The concern that no child should be left behind in their learning has also led to recognition that children with developmental delays or special needs should be identified early so that they, like other children, can benefit from their early experiences.

The latter has led to a focus on ensuring that every child makes progress in their learning relative to their different starting points and ages. Because of this, the importance of child development cannot be disregarded, since it is clear that if we want the best for children we must not only provide experiences that are appropriate for them but also, at the same time, there should be a focus on supporting them to achieve positive outcomes from their early education. Therefore the challenge for educators is how to support children's all round development whilst ensuring that they progress in their learning. Reinforcing the importance of this, studies in neuroscience and psychology identify the impact of early experiences on children's development – leaving no doubt about the consequences of neglecting to consider child development, and explaining the direction of travel of both current and previous governments when focusing on the area of children's life chances.

Findings, for example, from studies such as the New Zealand longitudinal research *Competent Children, Competent Learners* (Wylie *et al.*, 2011) which started in the mid-1990s, are beginning, some twenty years later, to reveal that children who were low achievers at 5 years of age did not go on to achieve the median scores for reading and maths when tested at 14 and 16 years of age, and that variables such as *'perseverance, communication and self-management'* (ibid.: 4) assisted those who went on at twenty to achieve in national tests. Other findings have firmly established that old thinking about nature and nurture are outmoded, and that whereas it was believed that genes and the environment acted independently of each other we now know that this is not the case and that experiences *'leave a chemical "signature", or epigenetic mark . . . which determines whether and how the genes are switched on or off'* (McCain *et al.*, 2011: 29) indicating that children's experiences contribute to how genes express themselves. This is summed up in a discussion of the impact of neuroscience on the current understanding of child development: *'children's environments and experiences mediate (either enhancing or diminishing) the potential with which children are born. In the past, it was commonly thought that intelligence was about 80% genetic and 20% environmental. Current thinking reverses the balance, that is, it is now thought to be 20% genetic and 80% environmental, with genes and experience being interdependent'* (Winter, 2010: 10). This indicates that effective teaching in the early years can have a huge impact on children's development and on their life chances.

A further consideration is that whilst babies' and young children's brains appear to be fully functional at birth this is not the case and it has been shown that *'The construction of neural (nerve) connections in the prefrontal cortex depends on childhood learning and is not complete until our 20s'* (McCain et al., 2011: 37). This is a strong reminder for parents of young children, and those who work with them, or lead schools and settings catering for them, of the powerful role of education in children's lives and for their life chances. It should be clear from these findings that knowledge of child development is essential to effective teaching and learning in the EYFS since it is known that what happens in the early years can build either a strong or weak foundation for a child's life and learning. A major consideration in this is that in the early years effective teaching and learning rely almost entirely on the nature of relationships, and research is very clear in asserting: *'Young children experience their world as an environment of relationships, and these relationships affect virtually all aspects of their development – intellectual, social, emotional, physical, behavioural and moral'* (National Scientific Council on the Developing Child, 2004: 1). How then do relationships contribute to teaching and learning in the EYFS?

How relationships contribute to teaching and learning in the EYFS, children's well-being and their capacity to be learners

When children experience positive relationships they are free to learn because their physiological and psychological needs are being met in the setting or school by the practitioner. This relationship is an attachment relationship. Attachment can be defined as: *'the continuing and lasting relationships that young children form with one or more adults'*, most particularly in relation to the *'child's sense of security and safety when in the company of a particular adult'* (Witmer, 2011: 2). Positive attachment experiences enable the young child to feel that *'I matter'* and *'I can make a difference'* (Miller, 2008: 2) and to focus his or her attention on exploring the environment and learning from experiences, interactions and encounters within it; conversely children who do not have this positive experience often focus their energies on trying to retain a connection with the adult, in order to get their needs met – however this is achieved. This frequently means the child is less able to interact with others or the environment because they are afraid to move away from the adult. A further by-product of this insecure attachment is that the child's ability to manage their changing emotions is reduced because they are not experiencing the reassuring and predictable responses that secure attachment provides. The physiological impact of attachment acts positively or negatively depending on the child's experiences and has been shown to affect the architecture of the developing brain, particularly in the first three years when brain development is at its most rapid.

It has been demonstrated that the benefits of primary attachments with the first carer (usually a family member) continue beyond the present moment, helping the child to develop trust in others, and an expectation that their needs will be met which supports them to develop socially. The consequences of early life stress, on the other hand, not only impact negatively on the child's emotions, expectations and beliefs about others' responses but also upon their long term health outcomes, exposing them to risky behaviour and issues such as reduced circulatory control and increased inflammation (Anda *et al.*, 2010). Reducing stress and improving children's well-being is relatively easy to achieve if practitioners are alert to children's emotional needs. Indeed several studies have shown that the significant factor that raises children's cortisol levels (known to elevate blood pressure, increase heart rate and blood sugar, and interrupt digestive and kidney functions) is not the absence of their primary caregiver but *'the absence of an adult figure who was responsive and alert to their states moment by moment'* (Gerhardt, 2004: 48).

This and other findings support the requirement in the EYFS for every child to be assigned a Key Person, though the description of this role does not present a sufficiently detailed or compelling argument in its favour. A more extended description of the role of the Key Person was presented in the EYFS (DfES, 2007) which identified the importance of the role in supporting secure attachment and children's independence. However, this may not have fully conveyed the continuing importance of the Key Person role beyond baby and toddlerhood into early childhood (three to six years of age), when children are still in need of positive relationships and are at greater risk of feeling insecure as they transfer from settings with higher adult:child ratios into settings and schools where the minimum ratio requirement is considerably lower.

One element of the Key Person role is responsiveness to children's feeling states; this relies on adults having the time and sensitivity to get to know and understand each child in their key group and consistently tune in to their signals. Building this relationship with the child takes time to achieve but is essential since it provides them with an acceptable alternative relationship from that of the main carer. It also reassures a child as they attend a new setting and supports them as they encounter many new adults and children. Describing a child as 'scared' of such encounters may sound extreme in discussions of their separation from a familiar carer but a young child's fear of abandonment can be intense and the need to rely on unfamiliar adults in schools and settings can be a frightening experience for a child of any age: it can be particularly daunting for pre-schoolers who often lack the ability to express their anxieties. A consequence of this is that children's behaviour becomes a means of externalising fear and can therefore be viewed as a form of communication.

Children's behaviour is a form of communication

Children's behaviour and responses reflect their experiences, for example, the child who has been affirmed for trying to do something independently, such as putting something away, continues to strive to achieve other accomplishments such as fetching a toy from another room, confident in the knowledge that they will receive further encouragement from their carer. Alternatively a child who learns to be wary of an adult's responses to his or her effort may either restrict their exploratory activity so as not to invoke a negative response or may engage in behaviours that achieve the carer's attention – even if the attention they receive is not positive.

Carefully and caringly observing children enables us to discover that their behaviour is acting as a marker to flag up their emotions – whether happiness, excitement or emotional turmoil; and though they may be unable either to recognise or verbalise this themselves, their behaviours tell us about how the child is feeling at a particular time.

Showing an interest in children's feelings helps them understand that their feelings are considered important. When practitioners enable children to discuss their feelings they learn that feelings are universal, acceptable and experienced by others as well as themselves.

Knowing that children's behaviour is a form of communication is a first step in understanding how to support their development; the next step is to identify what the behaviour is communicating and the final step is to support children to become resilient by helping them find ways of coping with feelings and emotions which they are finding difficult to deal with.

Enhancing children's vocabulary so that they are able to describe their feelings is recognised as a significant step in helping them to develop emotional intelligence; so for example using words to describe a baby's feelings validates them and their feelings and builds the child's repertoire of words allowing them eventually to express feeling states such as anger, hunger, sadness, excitement or tiredness. Sharing books that focus on feelings is also recommended since the child can identify with characters experiencing different emotions in response to events – sadness when something has been lost, anger when something has been snatched away or pleasure when a goal has been achieved.

A further way to support children's emotional responses when they are frustrated or angry is to teach them to stop before acting in the heat of the moment either by communicating to an adult that they are upset, or by methods such as slowly reciting numbers or rhymes aloud in order to stop themselves – often simply interrupting the feeling can help it to diminish though some children may need a great deal of help to understand that their response to certain feelings can be changed. This is an area discussed in more detail in Chapters 6 and 7. By developing strategies to help them recognise, understand and manage their feelings young children can be helped to become confident in themselves, sensitive to the feelings of others and more resilient.

How children develop resilience

Interest in the area of children's resilience has grown since the 1960s and 1970s because of concerns about children's mental health, particularly those children whose parents suffer from mental illnesses but also because of emerging findings from neurobiology about the influence of the early years for *'understanding and promoting resilience'* (Masten and Gerwitz 2006: 1). A simple definition of resilience used in *A Preschool Teachers' Manual* is *'an ability to recover from or adjust easily to misfortune or change'* (Baum *et al.*, 2005: 4). Discussing this subject a UK children's charity described resilience in relation to *'areas or "domains" of a child's life that can be manipulated or changed'* (Glover, 2009: 4); they cite the following intrinsic and extrinsic factors necessary to resilience. The intrinsic factors are:

- *'a secure base – the child feels a sense of belonging and security*
- *a sense of self-efficacy – a sense of mastery and control, along with an accurate understanding of personal strengths and limitations*
- *self-esteem – an internal sense of worth and competence.*

The extrinsic factors are:

- *at least one secure attachment relationship*
- *access to wider supports such as extended family and friends*
- *positive nursery, school and/or community experiences'* (ibid.: 4).

This suggests that when both intrinsic and extrinsic factors are in place the child is able to 'bounce back' because they have the internal capacity which is derived from the external support which most immediately affects their experiences. Describing these areas of influence, Urie Bronfenbrenner, a renowned developmental psychologist, whose work demonstrating the value of interventions in early childhood informed the establishment of the Head Start programme, identified layers which surround the child, beginning with the relationships the child experiences in his or her immediate family. This layer is surrounded by the mesosystem which describes those relationships beyond the family linking parents, family, work, the neighbourhood and other constant but less regular relationships which happen as part of living within a community (Siegler *et al.*, 2011: 367).

Whilst resilience is developed by many children even the most resilient are vulnerable to stress at times of transition or when other life-changing experiences occur, for example when a family member moves out of the home for a long period, or if somebody in the family is seriously ill. When very young children are fearful or anxious this is most often exhibited non-verbally, and some of the signs noted by doctors discussing pre-school children's responses show that whilst there are age variations in responses to stress the following reactions are typical:

- *'Clinging to parents or teaching staff*
- *Clinging to a favorite object such as a teddy bear or blanket*
- *Fears, either new or old*
- *Low threshold for frustration*
- *Crying and angry outbursts*
- *Regression to earlier stages of behavior*
- *Sleep and eating disturbances or changes'* (Baum *et al.*, 2005: 15).

These are the kinds of behaviour that are sometimes exhibited when children begin to attend a pre-school or school for the first time but they quickly disappear when the child receives reassurance and experiences empathy from their Key Person. The picture emerging of the continuum between resilience and vulnerability is that when children have a strong sense of belonging and identity and have secure attachments they can be supported to develop resilience and strategies to overcome life's adversities; whilst for children who do not receive this support the odds are often stacked against them which can lead to them experiencing a variety of difficulties, including mental health problems. Discussing children's resilience Ramon Lascano, who runs a project for children in the Andes, in South America, says: *'When children feel themselves valued for what they say, and see that others listen to them attentively, recognise the value of what they do, they develop self-confidence, and discover their self-esteem – a fundamental element in resilience'* (Lascano, 2004: 29). The revised EYFS is peppered with references to building children's self-confidence – this is a theme which is highlighted throughout this book. Its presence as a fundamental building block in the EYFS is intentional and indicative of the fact that policy makers now understand its importance not only for children but also for their future lives. The next section considers what has been discussed so far in this chapter in relation to the importance of child development to everyday practice.

Effective practice

Teaching and learning in the EYFS is founded on a complex web of relationships and children's sense of well-being and their capacity to learn is strongly linked to their emotional well-being throughout the EYFS, but particularly in periods of transition which can be experienced as stressful by children and parents if these are not well-managed. Transition practice should be constantly reviewed to ensure that settings work together to exchange information which will support each child's transition. This might involve sharing information and organising:

- visits from pre-school to school
- parent and child induction visits to school (as well as visits by teachers from the school to the setting);
- an album or booklet, that is shared regularly with the child by parents and pre-school/ school key person, containing photographs of any new practitioners the child will meet and the learning environment they are going to attend.

The role of the Key Person should also be reviewed so that particularly at the start of a transition period time is allocated to getting to know children as people (above anything else). This would involve practitioners being fully involved in children's play in order to gain an understanding of them and to build a trusting relationship with them. If children in the EYFS are to experience a sense of well-being it is essential that in each setting there is clarification of the depth and breadth of the role of the Key Person and an articulation of how practitioners will be supported to fulfil this role successfully. Being the Key Person for a young child can be a challenge for any number of reasons, therefore adults need significant support to carry out this role effectively.

Taking care of the well-being of adults in the setting is an important aspect of the role of leaders and managers who should ensure that practitioners can not only cope but also feel successful and rewarded in their work with children. Identifying one of the goals of education as encouraging children to be responsible and caring psychiatrist, Professor Adele Diamond points out *'we must ensure that teachers* [practitioners*] *are not so stressed that they are unable to provide caring role models for our children'* (Diamond, 2010: 781). In the process of supporting practitioners to provide caring role models leaders and managers might explore the following:

- Why the Key Person role was introduced and the compelling reasons for its continued retention as a legal requirement in the revised EYFS.

* Author's emphasis

- How the role can be developed so that children's well-being is always recognised as the first consideration, ahead of organisational and other demands.

Adopting this approach should alleviate some of the stresses placed on practitioners since without clarity about the purpose and importance of the Key Person role there can be confusion. Time spent in removing any such confusion will be worthwhile since *'Reducing stress in the classroom reduces teacher burn-out, improves classroom climate and leads to better educational outcomes'* (ibid.: 784). How does this happen? The emotional environment of any setting is created first and foremost by the adults who lead it and the teachers and practitioners who create it daily. When the adults in a setting are fully supported they focus on the needs of the children, recognising that every day is important for them.

Having their needs met and their feelings recognised and understood enhances children's self-esteem and boosts their prosocial behaviour, this feeds into the emotional environment of the setting: when children feel safe and secure they do not need to seek attention by presenting with challenging behaviours. The existence of clear boundaries identifying a few simple rules supports children's sense of being emotionally contained and their ability to develop resilience, since rules that are applied fairly and consistently help children focus on their own contribution to harmony in the setting. This atmosphere contributes to children's well-being which benefits them throughout their lives.

4   Engaging parents in children's learning

This chapter examines policy and issues for practice in the revised EYFS in relation to engaging parents of young children in their children's learning. It explores why parental involvement matters together with concepts of parental involvement and some barriers to engagement. It considers the requirement for parental engagement in the EYFS and ways of enabling parental involvement in schools and settings as well as practice in engaging parents. Throughout the chapter, research is examined, which offers compelling evidence about the importance of parental engagement and the home learning environment for children's outcomes, in addition to some constraining and enabling factors to effective practice in schools and settings in meeting the challenges of engaging and supporting parents in their children's learning.

Policy

Recent government policy recognises unequivocally the important role parents play in their children's learning, indicating: '*Mothers and fathers are their children's first and most important educators. From the moment of birth, the relationship between parents, and their child, and the activities they do together affect later development, giving children the trust, attitude and skills which help them to learn and engage positively with the world*' (DfE/DoH, 2011: 36). Furthermore a government funded review of best practice in parental engagement asserts: '*Parental engagement has a large and positive impact on children's learning. This was the single most important finding from a recent and authoritative review of the evidence*' (Goodall *et al.*, 2011: 3).

Considering further why parental involvement matters in early childhood a recent report indicated parents' involvement in their child's education is both '*a fundamental right and obligation*' (OECD, 2012: 2). This is recognised in the revised EYFS and as such enshrines this type of working practice as a requirement of providing early childhood education in England. Finally we are reminded that a further reason why parents should be involved in children's learning is: '*Parents and what they do have a powerful effect on children's learning . . . . . . key factors include a literacy rich home environment, quantity and quality of cognitive stimulation, parental sensitivity and child-centred emotional support and emphasis on the value of learning*' (Kernan, 2012: 6). Channelling this powerful source of support for children's learning must begin with defining what is meant by the term 'parental involvement'.

Concepts of parental involvement

A simple way of defining parental involvement is that it refers to '*the formal and informal relations that parents have with ECEC* [Early Childhood Education and Care] *services*' (OECD, 2012: 1); this will of course vary depending on the stage the child is at. When parental engagement is discussed in the literature it is often referred to in one or more of the following terms: '*family-school partnership, parental involvement, family involvement and parental engagement*' (ibid.: 1). However, there are many different models of engaging or involving parents – for example Pugh's model (Share *et al.*, 2011: 22) outlined five features of parental involvement in pre-school:

- *non-participation* – where parents choose not to be involved;
- *support* – where parents join in practically – perhaps by fundraising;
- *participation* – where parents are involved as helpers in the school, or as learners at a workshop for example;
- *partnership* – which is described in terms of parents being involved in a working relationship, and finally;
- *control*, where parents become decision-makers perhaps as school governors

Further typologies share some similarities (Evangelou *et al.*, 2008), whilst others discuss parental involvement as focusing '*on models for supporting parents in supporting their children's learning*' (ibid.: 7). These different perspectives were described in a government publication which identified two broad strands of parental involvement: '*Parents' involvement in the life of the school*' and '*their involvement in support of the individual child at home*' (DCSF, 2008b: 3). Though the relationship between these two positions is not discussed it can be seen that they may be connected, or even form a continuum, since some parents who become involved in the life of the school often then become 'switched on' to the bigger picture of the role they can play in supporting their child's learning, whilst others who support their child's learning at home may also find they have a contribution to make to the life of the school. However, it is argued, that the most important is the second of these; since there is *'consistent evidence of the educational benefits of involving parents in their child's learning at home'* (ibid: 3). Subsequent reviews of the benefits of parental engagement suggest that it is important to identify the most effective strategies for promoting parental engagement as well as finding ways of including *'those parents who are not significantly involved in their children's education or who are not involved at all'* (Goodall *et al.*, 2011: 3). This is seen as particularly important since the research indicates that *'What happens in the home environment has more influence on future achievement than innate ability, material circumstances or the quality of pre-school and school provision'* (DfE/DoH 2011: 36).

Rationale for developing the home learning environment

The weight of evidence supporting the importance of the home learning environment in children's education is profound – the reasons for variation in this tend to be associated with factors such as socio-economic status as well as the nature of parenting style and parenting skills. However, as indicated in a recent review of research, policy and practice in this area, early childhood education is *'not just about working with children it should also be about working with and supporting families'* because this promotes the well-being of children and gives them *'a good start to life-long learning'* (Kernan, 2012: 9). Amongst protective factors described in a research report key factors include:

- *'the quality of the early home learning environment*
- *attending a high-quality pre-school*
- *parental interest and involvement in early education'* (Siraj-Blatchford and Siraj-Blatchford, 2009: 17)

In further research on the role of the home learning environment on child development it was identified that *'if half or all of the 5 year old children who were read to less than daily were instead read to on a daily basis there would be corresponding 10% and 20% reductions in the proportion of 5 year olds with socioemotional difficulties'* (Kelly *et al.*, 2011: 5).

Reviewing the studies of interventions aimed at supporting parental engagement with children from 5–19 a DfE report (Goodall *et al.*, 2011) concluded that there is good evidence to show that literacy, numeracy and behavioural outcomes can be influenced through engaging parents effectively. However it also highlighted the importance of collaborating and engaging with parents, recognising their contribution and aiming to empower them through a sensitive approach, taking account of parents' needs, backgrounds, cultural norms and expectations. This approach is successful when settings and schools listen to parents' views, needs and anxieties in a non-judgemental way which invites and welcomes the voices of parents in the setting, acknowledging the strength of parental influence on children's beliefs, and attitudes about education and ultimately upon their outcomes.

However, although there are some fifty references to 'parents' in the EYFS, references to home learning are few and mainly related to issues arising from findings in relation to the assessment outcomes of children at aged two to three years, though brief reference is made to the role of the key person in supporting learning at home. Unfortunately one message that might be conveyed from this is that the revised EYFS is more focused on 'filling gaps' than on developing a proactive approach to exploiting the undoubted power of parents in their child's learning both throughout and beyond the EYFS, particularly since research findings show that parents want *'more information about what their children should be doing at different ages and stages and what activities parents can do at home'* (Hunt *et al.*, 2011: 9). However not all parents find it easy to become involved with a setting to support their children's learning because of a range of barriers.

Barriers to parental engagement

Amongst the least surprising factors that influence parental non-engagement are time constraints either because the child attends a pre-school setting for longer hours or because the parent works longer, in addition to the misconceptions of some parents who believe that once their child had started in a setting they are in less need of home learning opportunities – this was noted as particularly the case for *'Parents in families where no adult works full time'* (ibid: 9). Other obstructions to effective partnership are sometimes difficult to overcome – these include parental anxiety about settings, perhaps a left over from their own negative experiences in schools; lack of private space for meetings and/or the demands of caring for other children, as well as *'fear of being judged as a failing parent and past or on-going experience of discrimination'* (FPI website, 2013).

Additionally, restricted knowledge of child development can also be a barrier for less confident practitioners who can *'find it more difficult to share information with parents and may perceive parents' questions as a challenge to their professionalism'* (Share *et al.*, 2011: 38). This finding points to a number of key issues for continuing professional development, especially: the importance of a rationale for any parental partnership policy; support for practitioners in putting the policy into practice and the significance of communicating effectively, ensuring that all parents' concerns are suitably addressed.

Practice in engaging parents

In discussing ways of engaging parents in children's learning a research review points to the reciprocal effects of the child/parent relationship, stating: '*if children become more engaged in their learning this tends to encourage parents to do the same (and vice versa)*' (Goodall *et al.*, 2011: 86). When managers of early childhood settings were asked about how they involved parents in home learning – they identified three main approaches (Hunt *et al.*, 2011: 53):

- *General written information* (in the form of hand-outs or newsletters with information about home learning activities, EYFS implementation or lending of books and resources)
- *Involving parents in learning in the setting* (by inviting them to visit the setting, or to join in workshops, or to take materials home or to accompany staff and children on trips out)
- *Sharing information about their child's learning* (daily discussions or meetings or written feedback, including parental observations of their own child).

One starting point in enabling parental involvement is to ensure that there is a policy which defines important aspects of partnership – this will not exist in isolation from other policies but will be integral to many. An effective parental involvement policy will illustrate:

- the setting's philosophy in relation to the child in the context of the family
- the benefits of parents engaging in children's learning
- how the school or setting will support parents to engage in their child's learning at home and in the setting or school
- the role of the key person in engaging with parents
- the responsibilities and rights of parents and professionals in the process of supporting children's learning
- how the parental involvement policy relates to other policies – so, for example, a policy on transition would identify how partnership with parents would involve home visits at key points prior to and following the child's entry to a pre-school or school; whilst a policy on literacy would identify how parents would be supported to contribute to their child's learning in the aspects of speaking, listening, reading and writing.

After defining a policy a baseline of involvement can be measured focusing on levels of engagement in different groups or classes/across the setting or school and identifying the nature of involvement. An analysis of the baseline could then be developed into a series of goals expressing areas to be enhanced, identifying efforts to lead to a percentage increase in numbers of parents:

- Attending stay and play sessions
- Reading at home with their child
- Completing an activity or game with their child such as taking a photograph showing something the child enjoys doing at home;
- Completing a 'speech bubble' in words or pictures saying something about what the child has done at the weekend
- Attending a session to find out about developing children's early numeracy or literacy skills

These approaches are commonplace across schools and settings though many practitioners have expressed their concerns that these methods are not always as successful as they would wish. This suggests that the nature of interaction is extremely significant as well as the context in which it takes place. Some settings introduce activities which engage parents in ways not directly related to the child so that the sessions are viewed as 'person-friendly', acknowledging that the parent is a person first – these might include sessions offered on gender lines – such as 'dads and lads' events or those which offer social opportunities for communities where, for example, women's lives are devoted almost exclusively to family commitments. Such groups often provide opportunities for learning new skills such as attending language classes or developing computer skills. An expanding area which is increasingly used successfully in many settings and schools relates to the use of ICT – with many settings offering email alerts and information via a secure web-based platform, providing access to pages where class blogs can be viewed or where parents can add information about their own child's learning or development. Working respectfully with parents, whether communication is face to face, or electronic, involves developing relationships, inviting parents to make choices and respecting their views in a climate of trust and collaboration.

Establishing professional relationships is a necessary basis for engaging with parents – one highly regarded initiative which is premised on this, developed by the Pen Green Centre, is the Parental Involvement in Children's Learning approach (Pen Green, 2005). A review of this highlights the importance of a '*feedback loop*' between the home and the setting, encouraging all adults to be involved in the '*the process of "coming to know"*' and enabling parents and practitioners to '*become more aware of what they do so that they can become consciously more competent*' (Share *et al.*, 2011: 38). For both parents and professionals it is clear that understanding the significance of different aspects of children's learning is no small task. The process of engaging with parents adopted by Pen Green is beneficial for both parents and professionals since in working within such a framework practitioners develop their own understandings and can, as a result, support parents to develop theirs. This approach respects parents' greater knowledge of the child and allows practitioners and parents to share a professional language to discuss children's development, interests and learning. In this process parents are supported to recognise how children's behaviour indicates their levels of well-being and involvement (Pen Green, 2005) when undertaking particular activities, as well as identifying which schemas (ibid.) children are exploring at any time. By undertaking such an approach parents become confident that their knowledge of their own child is validated and they, in turn, become more conscious of their child's learning. This has many benefits which can transform the nature of interactions between the child and their parent(s) at home.

What do parents and practitioners mean when they talk about 'home learning' in the Early Years?

Parents and practitioners have different definitions of home learning. Whilst practitioners understand early home learning to be '*interaction between parent and child*' parents consider the definition to include learning through play, helping with domestic chores or outdoor activities (Hunt *et al.*, 2011: 9). This was identified in a study (ibid.) across 12 local authorities where all of the selected parent sample (558 originally) were found to be involved in some home learning with their pre-school child before they entered an EYFS setting. Interestingly, however, it was identified that these different definitions of home learning were important. One conclusion reached by the writers of this report indicates that a fundamental starting point for practitioners and parents should be to address the question: 'What does each group mean when they talk about home learning?' The definition proposed is contained in a list of seven activities described as the Early Home Learning Index (EHLI) based on findings from the EPPE research (Sylva *et al.*, 2004) which identified the following as associated with improved outcomes for children at ages three and seven:

- '*Parent reading to the child*
- *Parent taking their child to library*
- *Child playing with letters*
- *Parent helping child to learn the alphabet*
- *Parent teaching their child numbers or counting*
- *Child painting or drawing at home*
- *Parent teach their child songs, poems or nursery rhymes*
- *Visits and regular opportunities for play with friends at home*' (ibid.: 70).

The EPPE research found that these indicators of '*higher home learning environments were associated with increased levels of co-operation and conformity, peer sociability and confidence, lower anti-social and upset behaviour and higher cognitive development scores in children*' (Share *et al.*, 2011: 25). Importantly there is little information in the research which gives weight to the value of the things parents 'see' as educational, however, whether this is quantifiable or not is immaterial since just being with their parents and doing things together is known to be beneficial for children in terms of attachment and emotional development; so it is important that practitioners, whilst being clear about what works in terms of educational outcomes, are also encouraging of warm and loving relationships between parents and children. Furthermore a re-statement of the contribution of parents' perspectives on their children's learning and their contribution to the assessment of this is strengthened by recent EYFS Profile guidance which indicates: '*Reviews of the child's achievements should include those demonstrated at home as assessment without the parents' contribution provides an incomplete picture of a child's learning and development*' (STA, 2012: 11).

Effective practice

It has been demonstrated throughout this chapter that research findings show that involving parents can 'add value' to children's learning because of the benefits that accrue from this. These include social and emotional as well as cognitive outcomes. As has been discussed in this chapter the opportunities for engaging with parents are more extensive in the earliest years than at any other time in a child's life and it is these years which are known to be the most influential. At the same time the barriers to parental engagement can also be significant – and include constraints such as lack of time, limited access to transport and, for some parents, anxiety about entering educational establishments. Other constraints include cultural attitudes, organising time away from other children in the family, particularly babies and toddlers, and prioritising time to attend events in a setting or school, or to undertake activities that are known to promote children's well-being and learning.

One of the barriers which was also seen to militate against parental engagement in children's learning was practitioner resistance – and whilst the reasons for this may be varied – identifying the cause of this is vital if settings and schools are to succeed in harnessing support for young children's learning. Resistance may result from uncertainty; anxious practitioners may avoid dealing with some parents, effectively operating an unofficial 'closed door' policy. Often such reasons may seem real but are often perceptions based on a miscalculation. Involving parents fully, particularly when children are younger may lead parents to continuing engagement in their children's learning. It therefore makes sense to 'catch' parents at their most interested; when they are more willing to be involved, rather than distancing them through practices which have developed over time and have remained largely unquestioned.

What works in practice in the EYFS?

- Adherence to the principle of Enabling Environments – which recognises the importance of parental involvement in children's learning
- Building trust with parents through developing non-judgemental relationships
- Starting small and building on success – this might be verbal acknowledgement of what a parent describes about their child – developing over time into sharing discussions of how what has been discussed illustrates a child's learning.
- Sharing resources that might be scarce for some families – such as access to ICT; or use of a camera.
- Providing sessions which are not directly focused on children's learning but which involve parents in talking about their children and what they want for them.
- Offering resources such as games or story sacks to take home after providing sessions which help parents understand the purpose of the resources.
- Asking parents to talk about a picture of their child taken in the setting – this might be discussion of a two and a half year old who is confidently pouring water from a jug. The parent may explain that the child shows interest in the same thing at home.
- Valuing the expertise of parents in area such as gardening, cooking, art, storytelling or IT and inviting them to share skills.

When schools and children's centres or other feeder settings recognise that they are involved in a shared purpose practitioners and leaders can learn from one another, sharing expertise in ways that will benefit children, parents and professionals. However, since engaging parents in their children's learning is both a requirement in the EYFS, and recognised as essential for assessment at the end of the EYFS, this area is not optional so it should be considered a high priority for early years teams in all settings. It is the responsibility of senior staff to ensure that this works in practice by reflecting on their aims and purposes, together with fulfilling statutory requirements to develop policies that work in practice for the benefit of children and their families.

5 A pedagogy of care and education

Following many debates about the division between 'care' and 'education', a major marker reflecting changing attitudes to the education of young children in out of home settings in England was shown by the DfE/Sure Start in the development, launch and implementation of two frameworks for early years education in England. The first, published in 2000, was *Curriculum Guidance for the Foundation Stage* (QCA, 2000), a framework to support the learning of children aged from three to five. The second, in 2003, was a publication focused on the education of babies and younger children: *Birth to Three Matters* (DfES, 2003). Essentially what had been recognised by the UK government (and others) was that children's life chances were shaped largely by their earliest experiences and that early education was significant in contributing to these.

In the short period succeeding the publication of *Curriculum Guidance* and *Birth to Three Matters* a massive increase in state funding and an expanding 'childcare' sector led to discussions of a level playing field between private and maintained provision, and an early years curriculum that was continuous throughout a child's life from birth to five years of age. The outcome was the decision to amalgamate a number of documents bringing together 'care' and 'education' into a single approach in what became the Early Years Foundation Stage framework, first published in 2007 (reviewed in 2011 and re-published in 2012).

Beverley Hughes, MP, representing the UK at an international conference prior to this referred to *'a revolution in early years policy in the UK'* (Hughes, 2005) citing the first challenge as 'integration', stating: *'Evidence shows that bringing together care and learning will help all children, but particularly the most disadvantaged'* (ibid.). It is arguable that it was at this point that pedagogy crept into the cradle with the introduction of the EYFS 2007 in the words: *'The EYFS brings together and simplifies the learning and development and welfare requirements, in addition to ending the distinction between care and learning and between birth-to-three and three-to-five provision'*

(DfES, 2007: 10). This has left leaders, managers and practitioners to focus on how best to develop a pedagogy of care and education for babies and young children in ways that meet all their needs including supporting their emotional and cognitive development. However, whilst much has been understood about what is appropriate for young children in and out of home settings little guidance has been provided about the nature of 'pedagogy' and whether or how it is qualitatively different when children are very young. This is particularly relevant, when one considers the age range of children in the EYFS. Put amusingly, but appositely by Sir Ken Robinson there are *'several big bits to education'* which he describes as: *'the curriculum, which is what we want people to learn; then there's teaching, which is how we help them to do it; and assessment, which is how we make some judgments about how they're getting on'* (ABC website, 2009). The following chapters focus on these 'big bits' in the EYFS. To inform this consideration it is important to be aware that the learning requirements of the EYFS, which will be discussed are:

- *'the seven areas of learning and development and the educational programmes;*
- *the early learning goals, which summarise the knowledge, skills and understanding that all young children should have gained by the end of the Reception year; and*
- *the assessment requirements (when and how practitioners must assess children's achievements, and when and how they should discuss children's progress with parents and/or carers)'* (DfE, 2012: 4).

Whilst these requirements influence teaching and learning in the EYFS the EYFS is not, itself, a curriculum; it is simply a framework from which the curriculum can be constructed. This is similar to Australia where the Early Years Learning Framework is in place and educators are reminded that *'it is not a syllabus, not a program, not a curriculum, not a model, not an assessment tool, not a detailed description of everything a child will learn. It is a framework of principles, practices and outcomes with which to build* [a] . . . *curriculum'* (Australian Government, 2010: 3).

So, although the EYFS provides a curriculum framework offering direction about what children should learn and detailing specified outcomes the way these are to be achieved is not prescribed. This offers some degree of autonomy to settings and schools to build a curriculum which is based on the principles of the EYFS and which is in tune with their own philosophy and the children and families they serve. The way that practitioners teach is driven to a lesser or greater extent by the way the curriculum is perceived by leaders and managers and the expectations for children's learning – whether these are national expectations such as those that occur at the end of the

EYFS or expectations of 'norms' – stages children should reach in their learning at key points (often related to age).

According to educationalists discussing pedagogy in classrooms '*An imposed curriculum is apparent in language like "this is what we have to cover" whereas an emergent curriculum is apparent in statements like "what we are interested in"*' (Abbott and Edminston, 2006). The beliefs of practitioners and other influencers are therefore fundamental in determining whether an imposed or an emerging curriculum will take precedence – or, indeed, how a balance between the two will be struck, an area discussed in further chapters. Many would argue that with babies and toddlers it is possible to develop an emergent curriculum whilst, Alison Gopnik, professor of psychology at the University of California, Berkeley, suggests that, in later years '*Schoolwork revolves around focus and planning. We set objectives and goals for children, with an emphasis on skills they should acquire or information they should know*' (Gopnik, 2009), an approach which does not always provide the optimum conditions for children's learning since, she contends, children are explorers and are not constrained in their thinking in the same way as adults. Similarly, in a discussion of creativity and possibility thinking researchers found '*When the pedagogy is more visible and learning becomes bound by routines and framed by tight schedules, then the choice of learning activity is largely determined by the teacher and the child's sense of agency and volition is likely to be markedly reduced*' (Cremin et al., 2006: 12). This is an issue which reflective practitioners must engage with in order to strike an effective balance. In the next section definitions of pedagogy are considered and a working definition of pedagogy in the EYFS is offered to explore how learning and teaching can be integrated into a pedagogy of care and education with young children.

Pedagogy in the EYFS

One definition of pedagogy explains it as a: '*set of instructional techniques and strategies which enable learning to take place and provide*[s] *opportunities for the acquisition of knowledge, skills attitudes and dispositions within a particular social and material context*', referring to '*the interactive processes between teacher and learner and to the learning environment (which includes the concrete learning environment, the family and the community)*' (Siraj-Blatchford et al., 2002: 28). This definition is useful in as much as it stresses the wider dimensions of working within different contexts, different communities and with different families, however, it appears generic and could be applied to almost any teaching and learning context.

Another definition of pedagogy used in the Study of Pedagogical Effectiveness in Early Learning (SPEEL) research project is: '*Pedagogy is both the behaviour of teaching and being able to talk about and reflect on teaching. Pedagogy encompasses both what practitioners actually DO and THINK and the principles, theories, perceptions and challenges that inform and shape it'* (Moyles *et al.*, 2002: 5). This is a more extended definition which is a very useful guide for practitioners working within the EYFS and one which expands the previous definition.

One might think that the EYFS document itself would offer further insights into this area, however, whilst the revised EYFS refers to characteristics of effective teaching and learning little guidance is evident, in spite of the fact that during the Tickell Review it was revealed that practitioners were often confused about effective practice in teaching young children, leading the independent chair of the review, Dame Clare Tickell, to define teaching as: *'interacting with individuals or groups of children in ways which support their new learning, through a range of approaches within any context including play and planned activities'*, arguing further: *'Teaching approaches may include discussing children's ideas, providing language to name or describe, modelling, demonstrating, explaining, suggesting, questioning and encouraging as well as direct teaching of knowledge and skills'* (Tickell, 2011: 55). The revised EYFS does, however, discuss the role of play and provides some insights into the nature of adult involvement and interaction: *'Each area of learning and development must be implemented through planned, purposeful play and through a mix of adult-led and child-initiated activity. . . . Children learn by leading their own play, and by taking part in play which is guided by adults'* (DfE, 2012: 6). It suggests further, that whilst *'Practitioners must respond to each child's emerging needs and interests, guiding their development through warm, positive interaction. . . . There is an ongoing judgement to be made by practitioners about the balance between activities led by children, and activities led or guided by adults'* (ibid.: 6), going on to explain that as children mature and develop there will be a changing balance towards more adult-led activities, intended to: *'help children prepare for more formal learning, ready for Year 1'* (ibid.: 6). This recognises that relationships are important in early childhood education and appears to support professionals in judging what method of teaching and learning is appropriate for each child, even though it indicates that *'more formal learning'* is appropriate for children as they reach the end of Reception class.

Some dimensions of appropriate pedagogy in the EYFS are now considered based on analysis of the statutory document and in recognition that the EYFS relates to babies and young children. A working definition of pedagogy, for the purposes of this book, is proposed as:

Pedagogy is focused on meeting the needs of each child for safety, security and stimulation. It is based on positive relationships in enabling environments in which practitioners support each child's sense of self through interacting warmly with them, seeking to understand their current level of development and endeavouring to support them to take the next steps in their learning. They do this through developing a curriculum which meets the unique needs of individuals and is culturally sensitive and by supporting children's explorations, interests and play. They sensitively observe children and use observations and assessments to inform planning, structuring and resourcing the environment to meet children's changing needs over time.

The remainder of this chapter focuses on some of these aspects of pedagogy.

Meeting the needs of each child

Nowhere is the connection between emotional and cognitive harmony more significant than in the context of the learning and development of babies and young children, who learn about managing feelings and emotions through observing others, and interacting with role models such as parents, carers, family members and practitioners. The way pedagogy is developed in out of home settings with the youngest children is therefore highly significant because of the influence educators have on children's self-perceptions and attitudes throughout their lives. Indeed in a report of a dialogue between members of the Early Education Group about 'teaching', it was noted: '*in order to take on new challenges children need to be secure and to experience close and warm relationships with adults*' (Pascal, 2011: 1). This is important because it recognises that in the early years pedagogy relies heavily on relationships which intersect at different times and for different reasons – the threads of interaction occurring between:

- children and practitioners;
- children and children;
- practitioners and parents, and
- parents, children and practitioners.

With the youngest children interaction occurs through joint-involvement in daily events, in which process '*infants and their social partners intentionally focus on a common referent in the external environment*' (Siegler *et al.*, 2011: 162). This has been described as a 'dance' in which the participants move reciprocally – in tune with each other's state of mind and body language and there is a strong orientation of one to the other, indicative of the quality of attachment, between the practitioner and the child. As children mature involvement with others extends from the adult and one or two children into involvement in groups – greater adult:child ratios are maintained with younger children in order to facilitate their need for close contact with an adult. The exception is reception classes in schools which permit a ratio of one adult to thirty children – though most provide enhanced staffing and it is difficult to see how an appropriate experience could be provided if schools kept to the basic legal requirement.

Positive relationships in enabling environments

Research shows that the development of attachment with the practitioner is similar to the development of the primary attachment figure relationship but separate from it, suggesting that it is not simply an extension of this relationship, rather it is unique and can be developed independently. Findings also show that children develop attachment with a teacher when they spend more time with them *'and when the teacher is sensitive to children's needs'* (Raikes and Pope Edwards, 2009: 30). This indicates that children's development in out of home settings relies on both the quantity and quality of interaction and on the responsiveness of adults, particularly the Key Person to the child's communication signals, as well as on his or her attentiveness to their needs. Some of the behaviours demonstrated by sensitive teachers in relationship oriented programmes are helpful here in summing up the quality of interaction that is required to support young children's learning in all areas, visually:

- *'The teacher listens carefully to understand the child's communication.*
- *The teacher is warm and encouraging during interactions.*
- *The teacher gets on the children's eye level and maintains good eye contact with each child while interacting.*
- *The teacher is empathetic.*
- *The teacher is not harsh, intrusive, or punitive'* (ibid.: 11).

This approach is essential in the revised EYFS, where there is a renewed emphasis on supporting children's personal, social and emotional development, physical development and communication and language development. Therefore, the way that practitioners understand each child's current level of development in relation to each of these areas is crucial, as well as how these are applied through the Specific Areas.

Supporting each child's sense of self

Throughout our lives the influences of how our needs were met in early childhood continue to play a role in our expectations of life and of other people – from birth young children develop *'internal working models'* (Siegler, 2011: 426) or templates of how relationships work and those whose needs have been met develop the confidence to expect positive, timely responses from adults. Babies and young children need to feel physically and emotionally at ease, through experiencing nurturing behaviours that offer them a sense of being cared about. These caregiving practices offer reassurance to the child and reinforce their sense of self-as-important, in other words the child learns that somebody believes they are worth caring about, which in time leads the child to self-belief and to be able to care about others. This aspect of care is intended to be achieved in the revised EYFS through the role of the Key Person – and is just as important to children of four and five years of age as it is to babies and younger children.

A curriculum which meets the unique needs of the individual

The role of the adult in supporting babies' and young children's learning – is achieved in a variety of ways – but most importantly through developing a curriculum based on meeting the needs of individual children, ensuring it is culturally sensitive and through recognising that children's interests offer perspectives on their development. A starting point for considering the needs of individual children is to recognise the enormous variation in their experiences brought about by differences in family relationships, homes, material and economic circumstances, medical and social factors and linguistic, cultural and religious differences. Young children bring with them a unique set of expectations of the social world gathered from these experiences. Holding on to what they have learned from these differing experiences in comparison with what they must learn within the narrower and more homogenous context of the setting or school is both a challenge for them and for the setting they attend – particularly because at the beginning of their out-of-home experience what they know is strongly related to who they are and the differences they encounter may either lead them to embrace or reject that identity. Therefore teaching and learning plays a considerable part in supporting children to better understand their own and others' identities so that children develop self-respect as well as tolerance of 'otherness', whether that relates to gender, disability, culture, ethnicity, sexuality, religion, age or class/economic status.

Understanding children's development and supporting their next steps

There are parallels between the role of an early childhood practitioner and a scientific researcher – with each trying to find out about a subject and develop theories about it, before considering their interventions, which will lead to new learning about the subject (the child). The skill of the pedagogue is in taking account of the 'evidence' in a way that is sensitive to what the child brings from home; the key to supporting their development is to build a bridge by helping the child to 'make connections' in their learning. As indicated in the previous chapter, parents are the greatest resource in constructing a 'bridge' between the known and unknown; it is therefore important to ensure that the curriculum is responsiveness to children's prior experiences.

Sensitively observing children

As practitioners focus their attention on learning about children they can use what they know about the child to support planning for learning. They can also ensure that the environment enables the child to follow and expand his or her interests – these will change over time and as different explorations or lines of enquiry are discovered. As well as shaping and informing planning, observation also contributes to the assessments that are made throughout the time a child is in the EYFS.

Assessment

On-going assessment

Assessment is part of the observation and planning cycle – and occurs as part of daily interactions with children in their play. On-going assessment is what practitioners do as they 'think on their feet' about a child's learning. On-going assessments occur across all areas of learning and often involve several areas simultaneously – so a three year old child helping to set the table for lunch demonstrates both their physical skills as well as their mathematical understanding but may also reveal their personal and social skills – as they discuss with the practitioner why they like to be seated next to their friend. Therefore on-going assessments inform planning for children's learning and may lead practitioners to amend planning, in the light of new information. This approach demonstrates that whilst planning exists as a broad structure it is flexible enough to shape and direct children's learning, rather than acting as a tick-list of activities which must be 'achieved'. This suggests that plans may alter at times and that by deviating from written planning the changing direction of children's learning is recognised. On-going assessments should inform planning across all areas of learning in the EYFS for all children.

Assessing the child's learning – summative assessment – birth to three

Unlike on-going assessment, summative assessment does not occur on a daily basis, although it is drawn from on-going assessments. Summative assessment in the Prime Areas is built up over time and must focus, for the purposes of the Two Year Progress Check (NCB, 2012) on the following areas (Table 5.1) when a child is between 24 and 36 months of age.

At the end of the EYFS, when a child is in the final term of a reception class, summative assessment covers the areas and aspects of the Prime Areas in addition to the Specific Areas (Table 5.2).

Table 5.1 Focus of the Two Year Progress Check: Prime Areas

Personal, Social and Emotional Development	Self-confidence and self-awareness
	Managing feelings and behaviour
	Making relationships
Physical Development	Moving and handling
	Health and self-care
Communication and Language Development	Listening and attention
	Understanding
	Speaking

Table 5.2 Summative Assessment at the end of the EYFS includes the following in addition to the Prime Areas

Literacy	Reading
	Writing
Mathematics	Numbers
	Shape, Space and Measures
Understanding the World	People and Communities
	The World
	Technology
Expressive Arts and Design	Exploring and Using Media and Materials
	Being Imaginative

After completion in a setting of the Two Year Progress Check, during the period when a child is aged between 24–36 months, parents should receive 'a short written summary of their child's development in the prime areas' . . . . identifying 'the child's strengths, and any areas where the child's progress is less than expected' (DfES, 2012: 10). To support this, Development Matters provides materials for practitioners to:

- 'inform and support their assessment judgements of a child's development in the prime areas
- identify if there are any areas in which a child may be developing at a faster or slower pace than the expected level of progress for their age

> • *inform and support their discussions with parents and other professionals (where relevant)*' (NCB, 2012: 2).

If any concerns are raised at this point there is greater likelihood that intervention can impact positively on children's development. The re-launch by the National Children's Bureau of revised Early Support web-based resources may also be useful for assisting practitioners with meeting young children's identified needs (Nursery World website, 2013). These resources provide information to help parents track the development of children with special educational needs and disabilities (SEND) and may aid the development of a targeted plan (which is also a requirement) to support a child to make progress. Importantly, at no point should summative assessment focus on a deficit model, instead it should reflect on-going assessments identifying what the child can do and the next steps for development. It will be important to consider this holistically, taking account of what parents say about their child's development; what the child tells us about themselves – whether this is through verbal or non-verbal means; and what is known about the child from interactions with other children and people, including professionals who have some involvement with them for purposes such as physiotherapy, speech, language and communication or for any social or medical concerns.

Early Years Foundation Stage Profile (EYFSP)

On-going assessments also inform judgements which are reflected in the summative assessment of the outcomes of children's learning at the end of the EYFS, identified through completion of the Early Years Foundation Stage Profile (STA, 2012: 8) for each child in the final term of reception class. The EYFSP is underpinned by the following principles which should shape practice:

> • *'Reliable and accurate assessment is based primarily on the practitioner's knowledge of the child gained predominantly from observation and interaction in a range of daily activities and events.*
> • *Responsible pedagogy must be in place so that the provision enables each child to demonstrate their learning and development fully.*
> • *Embedded learning is identified by assessing what a child can do consistently and independently in a range of everyday situations.*
> • *An effective assessment presents a holistic view of a child's learning and development.*
> • *Accurate assessments take account of contributions from a range of perspectives including the child, their parents and other relevant adults'* (ibid.: 8).

There are 17 early learning goals (ELGs) that must be assessed for each child in completing the EYFSP – these reflect the outcomes of learning for the eight aspects of the Prime Areas (Table 5.1) in addition to the eight aspects of learning in the Specific Areas (Table 5.2)

The EYFSP requires that practitioners review their knowledge of each child using information from all sources to make judgements about whether their achievement of each ELG is best described as one of the following:

- *'the description of the level of development expected at the end of the EYFS (expected);*
- *not yet at the level of development expected at the end of the EYFS (emerging); or*
- *beyond the level of development expected at the end of the EYFS (exceeding)'* (STA, 2012: 11).

Alongside this information there should be a narrative description for parents and teachers in the receiving Year One class of how a child learns – this is a commentary of one or two paragraphs identifying how the child demonstrates what the EYFS describes as the key characteristics of effective learning. A more detailed description of these characteristics is offered in the EYFSP, these are also discussed in a later chapter.

Together, the Prime Areas and Specific Areas form the basis of the EYFS curriculum, however, unlike the Prime Areas of the curriculum, which mainly focus on children's development, the Specific Areas underpin later subject learning in school, shaping children's attitudes to some of these, as well as creating the foundations for later learning. In view of this it is important to ensure that learning is an inspiring and enriching process which children experience through their play and through teaching interactions which are appropriate to their development and which give them the desire to learn and the motivation to continue learning well beyond early childhood. Therefore learning should always be planned in consideration of the child's characteristics as a learner as well as in the context of maintaining each child's self-confidence, since self-belief is central to successful learning. This is especially important because: *'Early mastery experiences are predictive of children's cognitive development, and there is evidence to suggest they work independently of critical variables such as socioeconomic status'* (Pajares and Schunk, 2002: 23). Pedagogical decisions in the early years focus on facilitating children's learning through drawing on a range of skills and attitudes discussed in this chapter and throughout this publication, helpfully summarised in Table 5.3.

The next chapter focuses on teaching and learning in the Prime Areas with children from birth to three.

Table 5.3 Interactions for scaffolding learning (Queensland Studies Authority, 2006: 66)

Types of Interaction	Examples
Facilitating children's learning through:	• Modelling and demonstrating techniques and strategies • Using teachable moments • Providing opportunities for choice • Supporting child-initiated explorations, investigations and play • Providing supportive feedback on attempts and approximations • Adjusting interactions to enable children to demonstrate different outcomes within particular learning contexts • Breaking down tasks and prompting for the next step • Providing environments for independent and collaborative learning • Involving partners in facilitating learning.
Collaborating as a learning partner by:	• Collaborating and working alongside children • Inquiring and investigating together • Involving other partners in the learning and decision making • Celebrating successes together • Negotiating and collaboratively planning projects and experiences • Listening to children and responding to their questions and ideas • Co-constructing understandings • Communicating what children are learning to other partners.

Making learning explicit by:	• Making language and thinking strategies explicit • Discussing and explaining meanings and ideas • Directing attention to important aspects of the situation or task • Engaging with, using and responding to texts • Verbalising and modelling thinking and problem-solving
Building connections by:	• Drawing on children's prior knowledge and making links to new experiences • Assisting children to make connections between experiences • Drawing children's attention to learning and everyday situations in which learning is used • Identifying features, similarities and differences • Gathering information from other partners to help build connections between home, communities and classrooms.
Extending children's thinking to develop deep understandings through:	• Questioning to support children as they examine bias and stereotyping • Challenging children to consider other points of view and practices • Including diverse ideas, perspectives and alternatives • Extending children's thinking through using a variety of open-ended questions • Assisting children to reflect and evaluate • Developing a language for talking about thinking and how we know and understand the world • Questioning children to help them verbalise their thinking or explain how they know • Assisting children to pose and solve problems • Engaging children in imagining and generating possibilities • Engaging in substantive conversations with children • Involving other partners in building the intellectual quality of learning experiences.

6   Teaching and learning in the Prime Areas: Birth to three

This chapter will focus on pedagogy in practice with children from birth to three in the Prime Areas of the EYFS:

- Communication and Language (C&L)
- Physical development (PD), and
- Personal, Social and Emotional Development (PSED)

The following chapter will then consider the same areas with reference to the experiences of three, four and five year olds. There will inevitably be some overlap between the two since although children are often organised in same age groups the development of children in any one age group may be closer to that of older or younger children. Whilst in practical terms pedagogical approaches in the EYFS may be different dependent on the setting and the child's developmental stage, they will nevertheless be consistent in recognising the child as a competent learner from birth with the capacity and motivation to learn when appropriate experiences are provided. This is achieved when the principles of the EYFS are put into practice. It involves practitioners in:

- undertaking observations to establish children's current interests and level of development;
- planning for children's play and learning;
- planning the environment for learning;
- assessing children's development and learning, and
- planning for the next steps in children's play and learning.

With younger children these processes may not be evident as separate steps since practitioners rarely set out to teach a particular skill or concept at any given time because learning usually emerges as the outcome of a process rather than from following a precise plan. However, there will be times when practitioners focus on facilitating certain learning through modelling skills or actions and through interacting with a child in a shared aim. Pedagogical responses can take many forms – these will relate to areas discussed in previous chapters as well as:

- the needs of each child at particular times
- an understanding of how children learn
- presentation of the environment and resources to enable all children to participate fully, and
- decisions practitioners make about the focus of their work;

Contexts for learning from birth to three

Children's learning occurs everywhere and their self-initiated play provides many occasions when learning may occur. Therefore being alert to such possibilities is essential – in order to capitalise on 'teachable moments'. This means that although some planning is necessary it should not constrain flexibility. The way early learning environments are prepared clearly influences children's urge to investigate and explore. Ideally these should be available both in and out of doors throughout the year and as well as being intriguing should also be safe, well-maintained and carefully managed. Central to children's learning is the role adults assume, playfully interacting with children, sometimes following their lead and at other times leading the child's learning in a particular direction. Provocations for such learning can arise from the smallest stimulus and may also be inspired by any or all of the following:

- **Children's experiences at home** shared by parents with the setting, for example the child who has been to a soft play session may have a new-found interest in climbing; or one who has attended an event such as a puppet show may be keen to re-enact the experience.
- **Visits or visitors the setting has arranged** – this may involve a trip to a farm centre which may increase children's interest in animals which could then be extended through small world play and books and the setting up of a 'veterinary' play area.
- **A child's interest – this might be in any number of things such as bags, bubbles or babies** – these may last for a short period or may continue over days, or longer. Supporting these should not be to the exclusion of all other things.
- **Play with words, sounds, language, music** – this happens from the first weeks after birth and by 6–8 weeks young babies are vocalising and communicating more and more. The adult acts as a listener, a role model, story teller, game player, singer or a partner in conversation, dependent on the baby or young child's lead. For

toddlers, the repertoire is extended and they are able to repeat and join in with refrains, sometimes stopping in anticipation as the chorus or final words are sung or said.

- **Heuristic play, treasure baskets or playing with finds, or found materials** – Heuristic play was a term coined by Elinor Goldschmied who believed that through '*exploring the properties of everyday objects or cultural artifacts, in a safe, supported, open-ended manner*' young children were given a chance to '*determine their own actions and make choices*' (Auld, 2002: 36). Through the provision of items made of wood, metal or other materials and allowing the child to explore freely they find out what the object is, as well as discovering properties such as whether something is cool or warm to touch, knobbly or smooth, heavy or light.

- **Pretence, imagining or transforming items** – sometimes the introduction of an item or a piece of material can be a trigger for pretending one thing represents another – so a rectangle of material can become a cover for a den, or a Spiderman cape; or a carton might become a place to hide or to keep a soft toy, whilst a large tube may become a telescope or a track for cars.

- **Repeated activity** – plastic bottles might be transported from shelf to table or a child might fill a bag with certain items or 'post' items or enclose one item inside another. Explained as 'schema', these repeated play patterns offer an insight into the child's pre-occupations and when understood as patterns of play can be facilitated by thoughtful planning.

- **Mark-making, painting, sticking and gluing** – these begin as exploratory behaviours which become more intentional as the child's planning skills are supported and their physical capabilities grow; young children often simply want to explore the properties of materials. They are often fascinated by the way glue adheres to paper or become engrossed in making marks on page after page of an old magazine, for example.

- **New skills children are developing** – for example the toddler who is learning how to jump with both feet – facilitating this development will take priority over other things simply because the child's drive towards achieving this skill is so strong.

Beyond this the environment will offer a broad range of opportunities for young children to engage in many different types of play, interaction and learning. Provision and resources will be extended or altered in keeping with children's ages and interests. Areas for quiet activities such as looking at books, observing the rest of the room, talking or listening will be accommodated alongside those which offer opportunities for physical exploration and open-ended activities which allow children freedom to find out about objects and materials in the environment. These are usually available through:

- **Areas of provision in and out of doors** offering variations because of the way these are organised from setting to setting – many providing for exploration and investigation in play with water and sand; dens, tunnels, malleable materials; books; creative and imaginative role play; construction; mark-making; movement and dance; making and doing and physical play.
- **Displays and invitations to experiential centres** (Saskatchewan Ministry of Education 2008: 60)– these are often called investigative areas and might be connected with exploring and investigating: motion; light, colour and shadows; sounds and natural and living things.

Clearly this is not an exhaustive list – it is essentially intended to reflect the fact that learning happens everywhere and occurs through both planned and unplanned experiences. How the environment is organised is a matter of choice and whilst many settings offer a similar arrangement others provide an eclectic mix of areas blending into each other. Importantly, resources should be set out so that children are able to access them independently.

Adult involvement in children's play

In order for the different contexts for learning to be successful adults need to be involved at some level – this may be in any of the following ways:

- Observer of the play
- Partner in the play
- Facilitator of the play
- Resource provider

A further significant pedagogical issue is creating the 'balance' between child-initiated and adult-led activity which is a requirement in the EYFS; how to achieve this balance cannot be prescribed since the decision is based on both professional judgement and common sense; however, the younger the child, the greater the balance towards child-initiated activities.

Young children's learning

The characteristics of effective learning referred to previously should be considered in making decisions about children's learning. These are fundamental characteristics of young children which emerge when their physiological and psychological needs are met – and in thinking about young children's learning it will be important to consider these as part of the observation process so that children's attitudes and responses are understood and supported effectively. The characteristics of effective teaching and learning (DfE/EE, 2012: 6–7) are presented in Table 6.1.

Table 6.1 The characteristics of effective learning

The Characteristics of Effective Learning		
Playing and Exploring (Engagement)	**Active Learning (Motivation)**	**Creative and Thinking Critically (Thinking)**
Finding out and exploring • Showing curiosity about objects, events and people • Using senses to explore the world around them • Engaging in open-ended activity • Showing particular interests	**Being involved and concentrating** • Maintaining focus on their activity for a period of time • Showing high levels of energy, fascination • Not easily distracted • Paying attention to details	**Having their own ideas** • Thinking of ideas • Finding ways to solve problems • Finding new ways to do things
Playing with what they know • Pretending objects are things from their experience • Representing their experiences in play • Taking on a role in their play • Acting out experiences with other people	**Keeping on trying** • Persisting with activity when challenges occur • Showing a belief that more effort or a different approach will pay off • Bouncing back after difficulties	**Making links** • Making links and noticing patterns in their experience • Making predictions • Testing their ideas • Developing ideas of grouping, sequences, cause and effect

Being willing to 'have a go'	Enjoying achieving what they set out to do	Choosing ways to do things
• Initiating activities • Seeking challenge • Showing a 'can do' attitude • Taking a risk, engaging in new experiences, and learning by trial and error	• Showing satisfaction in meeting their own goals • Being proud of how they accomplished something – not just the end result • Enjoying meeting challenges for their own sake rather than external rewards or praise	• Planning, making decisions about how to approach a task, solve a problem and reach a goal • Checking how well their activities are going • Changing strategy as needed • Reviewing how well the approach worked

Development in learning

An additional way of thinking about young children's learning is proposed in the guidelines referred to in the previous chapter, which suggest that there is a predictable sequence in young children's learning throughout the early years, visually:

- the child becomes aware,
- the child explores,
- the child makes connections in their learning, and
- the child then applies what they have learned, which takes their learning beyond the original level (Queensland Studies Authority, 2006: 21).

This approach is presented in Table 6.2 which provides examples of the child's responses at each of the four stages and identifies areas for observation at each stage together with suggestions of what adults might do to support children's learning through contingent interaction. This sequence is useful in analysing practice in relation to a child's development and helpful in identifying:

- whether a child is at an **awareness or entry stage**, in which they are perhaps focused on doing familiar things, such as enjoying repetitive stories, rhymes and routines; or

Table 6.2 The phases of learning and development (Adapted using: Queensland Studies Authority (2006: 71)

Phase of Learning and Development	Child's Response	Observational Focus	Interactions that Promote Learning
BECOMING AWARE – in which children:	• *'rely on their personal observations and habitual behaviour* • *need explicit support to engage with new learning* • *use their learning in limited contexts'*	This phase is concerned with the here and now and is heuristic, experiential and random, though connections are being made as the child attends to *'new things in their lives'.*	*'Teachers provide explicit support to explain new learning to children and make links to their prior learning'.*
EXPLORING – in which children:	• *'Construct personal understandings* • *Need support to engage with new learning* • *Use their learning in familiar contexts'*	Exploring new objects, situations, activities and finding out about others.	*'Teachers provide support to extend children's personal understanding'.*
MAKING CONNECTIONS – in which children:	• *'Make connections between their personal understandings and commonly accepted understandings* • *Need some prompts to engage with and talk about new learning* • *Are beginning to transfer their learning across familiar contexts'*	Children's own ideas become evident as they express themselves using different media – so a few lines may represent a dragon, or marks may be given meaning.	*'Teachers provide prompts or brief interactions to help children make connections between their personal understandings and commonly accepted understandings'.*

| APPLYING – in which children: | • 'More readily recall and explain their conceptual understandings • Apply their knowledge of the new learning independently • Confidently transfer their learning across familiar contexts' | In this phase children are able to consider their own intentions and plan what they intend to do as well as to reflect on their learning. | 'While children can independently apply their understandings and capabilities, teachers interact with them to deepen and further their understanding' (ibid.). |

- at an **exploratory stage** where they are beginning to try new things perhaps choosing to sit next to a new friend, try a new food, play in different areas; or
- whether they are **linking what they already know to a new situation** – for example recognising, though not necessarily verbalising, that throwing bean bags is similar to throwing balls; or
- whether **applying new learning to** a different situation, or to explain something – for example: having planted seeds before, they know they must be watered and kept warm.

Obviously, this is an iterative process; as children reach new understandings in any element of their learning they need new provocations to motivate them to become motivated and engaged in new learning.

How does everyday practice support children's learning in the Prime Areas?

In order to support children's learning in the Prime Areas it is essential that practice is focused on all aspects of learning in each of the three areas. Additionally, partnership work with children's parents is vital, since by working with parents practitioners can compare their own observations with what parents say about their child's learning and development to arrive at a more accurate conclusion about the child's current development and the next steps for their learning. They can then plan experiences which match children's interests and structure and resource the environment to meet children's changing needs over time. The connection between the Prime Areas is underscored in *Development Matters* where it is stated that the practitioner may observe the baby responding *'when talked to, for example, moves arms and legs, changes facial expression, moves body and makes mouth movements'* (DfE/EE, 2012: 8). This describes how the baby communicates as much as how the baby is feeling and, in addition, tells us about the baby's developing physical skills. This interconnection between the Prime Areas should be borne in mind at all times; however for the purposes of this and the next chapter, each is considered separately.

In the Practice Reviews that follow, short examples of child/adult interaction are set out in relation to each of the eight aspects of the Prime Areas. Each vignette provides a description of a short encounter of the type observed in everyday practice with young children; the purpose, in offering these examples, is to highlight the nature of what pedagogy might look like in practice with very young children and to offer pause for reflection about both its nature and significance. Reference to the scenarios described will also illustrate the nature of involvement, referred to earlier in relation to the adult's role in children's play. The sections, which follow each vignette are intended to offer a lens for reflection on:

- Everyday Practice
- Questioning Everyday Practice
- Effective Practice

Possible pedagogical responses are considered in relation to each vignette – none of the responses is proposed as being correct or incorrect – they are simply examples of the types of responses observed in different settings over a period of years. These are presented as:

- (a) reactive responses – which may occur when attention to the aspect of learning has not been thoughtfully considered
- (b) partial responses – which may occur when the aspect of learning is not fully thought out
- (c) considered responses – which occur when opportunities are taken to capitalise on significant aspects of learning

Their purpose is to prompt discussions about the nature of pedagogy, and about how relationships support the child in their sense of being understood and valued, an entitlement for every child in the EYFS. Following each short case study the characteristics of learning are briefly considered in relation to each child. To analyse the responses further a more in-depth understanding could be developed by comparison with guidance such as that presented in the Revised Infant Toddler Environmental Rating Scale (ITERS-R) (Cryer *et al.*, 2004).

COMMUNICATION AND LANGUAGE (C&L)

C&L comprises three aspects:

- Listening and Attention
- Understanding
- Speaking

When we focus on the aspects of C&L in Figure 6.1 it is easy to see how each is dependent on the other and whilst they are discussed separately here none should be considered more important than any other because they are interdependent.

Through listening and attending to sounds in the environment, particularly language sounds, the young child begins to acquire an understanding of significant sounds in the language or language(s) spoken in the home by parents or carers and in the setting by practitioners and other children. The complexity and range of sounds a child may hear should not be underestimated since although there are 44 phonemes (units of sound) in English, there are many regional variations on these – for example – the 'a' sound changes from North to South. Furthermore, in England many other languages are spoken – and, in Manchester, now thought to be the most diverse city in the UK for spoken languages, there are reported to be as many as 153 languages in use in schools (MEN Media website, 2012). This serves as a reminder of the significant role practitioners play in supporting not only young children's linguistic diversity but also their cultural heritage.

Increasingly research evidence shows that understanding language and having a wide vocabulary are significant indicators of children's future successful learning in literacy, mathematics and other areas. Several recent studies in Canada suggest that *'After birth early language exposure at home predicts the size of children's growing vocabulary and later verbal skills and literacy skills'*, identifying that: *'One U.S. study stated that by age 4, children in affluent families have heard 30 million more words and have vocabularies that are three times larger than children in low-income families. Children with poor verbal skills at age 3 are likely to do poorly in language and literacy when they enter school, and many go on to have poor academic careers'* (McCain *et al.*, 2011: 38). So what is involved in speaking or expressive language in the first years?

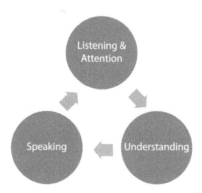

Figure 6.1 The inter-related aspects of Communication and Language

Speaking is about making the journey from generating random sounds and using body language to using words or signs with intentionality to convey meaning. In a detailed description of children's communication skills the author, Belinda Buckley, in what she describes as the *'transition towards purposeful sounds'* (Buckley, 2003: 43) describes babies' turn-taking with others in the production of sounds and their listening for responses as part of a continuum involving:

- babbling (repeated strings of sounds), towards
- jargon where different vowel sounds are introduced when sentence like, though mainly incomprehensible lengthy speech-like sounds are produced; these foreground the production of:
- protowords (these are defined in terms of children's *'consistent and intentional use . . . of idiosyncratic sound patterns'* (Buckley, 2003: 231).

Whilst the next phase of communication is about:

- developing understanding and production in speech of real words, phrases and sentences to convey a range of ideas, feelings, meanings and thoughts.

Practice review C&L 1: Listening and Attention

The focus of listening and attention at the end of the EYFS is set out in the Early Learning Goal (ELG) for this aspect, which is for children to listen attentively in a range of situations, responding to what they hear with relevant comments, questions or actions, giving their attention to what others say and responding appropriately, while engaged in another activity. The starting point for this journey begins with incidental discussions and involvement with adults and other children which focus the child's attention, especially when verbal or physical cues are provided.

Everyday practice

Consider the pedagogical responses below:

Holly, who is 14 months old is seated in her high chair looking very interested in receiving the fruit (part of her breakfast) which she really enjoys eating – she claps her hands and squeals with delight when it is passed towards her.

a) The practitioner says: '*Raspberries – yeah! You're favourite, Holly*'. S/he then remarks to another staff member: '*We've not had these for ages, have we? Holly really loves them!*'

b) The practitioner says: '*You're all excited, aren't you? I know, it's your favourite today and you'll eat it all up!*' Smiling at Holly who begins eating the raspberries, s/he then turns to wipe a spot where the bowl has made a wet ring. Turning back to the child s/he says: '*Good girl, you're eating your raspberries all by yourself, aren't you?*' S/he then quickly makes a note in Holly's home diary that Holly has enjoyed a good breakfast.

c) The practitioner says: '*Look Holly*' pointing to the bowl '*do you remember what they are?*' S/he pauses to ensure that Holly is listening and in response to the child's attention says: '*They're raspberries, aren't they? Raspberries!*' S/he says lifting a raspberry and placing it next to a picture of the fruit nearby. Holly murmurs a sound like '*ss*' and smiling begins to eat the fruit. '*Raspberries are your favourite, aren't they?*' the practitioner comments, as the child carefully eats the fruits. S/he then smiles saying: '*Only two left now, Holly, soon they will be all gone!*'

Questioning everyday practice

Holly's learning characteristics:

Holly is curious and excited about the anticipated arrival of the raspberries in the dish – this indicates she is engaged and '*showing curiosity about objects*' (DfE/EE, 2012: 6) an example of Playing and Exploring, one of the characteristics of effective learning. She is also confident to feed herself and appears to be at home in the setting.

Pedagogical response review

In (a), the reactive response, the practitioner has labelled the fruit and acknowledged that it is the child's favourite. S/he has also used the child's name, important in gaining her attention. However, rather than waiting for the child's response s/he has become distracted and has not followed the conversation through. In (b), the partial response, the practitioner has indicated s/he is aware that raspberries are Holly's favourite fruit and smiling at Holly has conveyed warmth and recognition; s/he has also commented positively on the little girl's independence. In (c), the extended response, the practitioner has treated Holly as a communicator. This is encouraging for Holly; the practitioner has also followed the child's lead by using carefully chosen words that are meaningful and which will encourage Holly to listen to what s/he is saying – this includes using the child's name: 'Holly'; s/he has also labelled the fruit: 'raspberries' and Holly has repeated an approximation of the word, by saying '*ss*'. The practitioner has offered a commentary on the child's actions which also encourages understanding. This exchange would be likely to increase Holly's desire to interact with adults (and children).

Consciously focusing on supporting the child's communication and language development in routine activities should be planned as part of a wider strategy for developing children's communication and social skills.

Effective practice: Experiences which support listening and attention

- **Creating places, spaces and opportunities** for children to listen to and to join in with songs, rhymes, stories, music and verse.
- **Talking in a whisper or a quiet voice**; or telling a story with a different tone of voice for each character – this inspires children's interest and their desire to imitate what they have heard.
- **Including props alongside a story** to draw children in; the addition of resources such as puppets to represent characters in a story can increase listening time.
- **Commenting routinely** in everyday situations such as when a child is playing in the mud or noting how a child is balancing two objects on top of one another, or talking about the child's choice of food at meal times.

These types of interactions support the young child's receptive language (what he or she understands but cannot express verbally) and leads to the development of expressive language (speech and communication skills).

Practice review C&L 2: Understanding

The focus of Understanding at the end of the EYFS is set out in the Early Learning Goal (ELG) for this aspect, which is that children follow instructions involving several ideas or actions, and answer 'how' and 'why' questions about their experiences and in response to stories or events. This begins with every encounter when joint-involvement between adults and children, and between children and children, is recognised as meaningful. Opportunities to increase early understanding occur in everyday play contexts where playful interactions focus children's attention on understanding.

Everyday practice

Consider the pedagogical responses below:

Noah, almost two years old, walks into the book area, finds a book: *The Baby Dances* (Henderson, 1999) and turning towards the practitioner says: *'mummy, baby, stairs'.*

a) The practitioner responds by saying *'You like this one, don't you?'* Then, not expecting an answer to his question he raises his arms above his head and says: *'Can you dance, like the baby, Noah?'* Noah looks away. Taking his hand the practitioner says *'Come on then, shall I read it to you?'* and sitting down with Noah he opens the book and begins to read. Noah sits motionless beside him.

b) The practitioner responds by looking at the book and says animatedly *'Do you want me to read it to you, Noah?'* The toddler nods. The practitioner leads him to a cosy spot and says: *'Alright, let's sit down then'.* He and Noah look for a moment at the picture on the front cover, the practitioner asking *'Is your baby like that?'* but before Noah has chance to reply the practitioner turns to the first page of the story and begins reading the words: *'The baby's born. The baby's born'* (ibid.: 1), pointing to the pictures. He occasionally looks at Noah to check that he is still interested as he is very still though he appears involved.

c) The practitioner says to him – *'Yes, you're right, this book is about a baby –You've got a baby haven't you, at home, and your baby is sometimes upstairs with mummy, isn't he?'* He pauses to give him time to show his understanding and after a short while he nods, smiling up at him. He then says: *'Are you saying "Yes"?'* and Noah says *'Yes'* in response. *'Shall we sit down and get comfy, so that we can enjoy this story?'* When they are settled he asks Noah: *'Is that baby like your baby, Noah? Is it like baby Joel?'* The toddler looks at him repeating the words 'baby' and 'yoer', the practitioner says looking at him: *'Yes! You think he's like baby Joel'.* When they have finished looking at the picture he asks the little boy to help him turn over the pages the practitioner commenting on all that the baby is able to do as she grows into a toddler. Occasionally Noah points to the pictures and the practitioner then comments on what Noah has pointed to, sometimes asking a question and giving him enough time to answer. He then often repeats or re-casts what he has said to confirm for Noah that he has understood his responses. After reading the book the practitioner suggests Noah might like to look at pictures of baby Joel in his 'My family' album.

Questioning everyday practice

Noah's learning characteristics:

Noah is aware of books and stories and like Holly he is also actively engaged. He initiated the activity, which suggests he is willing to '*have a go*' (DfE/ EE, 2012) an example of Playing and Exploring, one of the characteristics of effective learning. He is also developing language and communication skills since he is putting several words together to convey meaning.

Pedagogical response review

In (a), the reactive response, the practitioner is relating to the child, though the speed with which he starts his 'dance', and his expectation that Noah would not answer him, diminish opportunities for Noah to show his understanding. The fact that Noah looked away, may convey he feels uncomfortable. In (b), the partial response, the practitioner has responded pleasantly to the toddler, and is also encouraging of his choice and respectful of his request to share the book. Whilst he has obviously been quick to respond to the child's request he has overlooked the importance of giving Noah a chance to reply verbally because he has simply taken his nod of the head as a 'yes', rather than offering the word 'yes' as a model for him to hear. By pointing to the baby and naming the different actions that are demonstrated he is supporting the toddler's understanding. In (c), the extended response, the practitioner has shown Noah that his communication has been recognised as meaningful because he connects his choice of book with the arrival of his new baby at home. By offering this information to Noah the practitioner is helping him remember important pieces of information; giving him time before answering questions for him he provides 'thinking space' so that he can decide what he wants to say.

A focus on the child's development of receptive language should be integral to every interaction. Discussions of pictures, places, events and characters in stories can provide a meaningful context for developing children's Understanding.

Effective practice: Experiences which support Understanding

- **Engaging in dialogic book talk** – when a baby or young child and an adult share a book the adult scaffolds the child's learning through talking about the book and asking open-ended questions which provide a context for the young child's thinking. Allowing time for the child to respond is important; as the child becomes confident in exploring the story they may ask questions and when very familiar with the story they may 'read' it to the adult.
- **Talking to the child about what is happening and asking them about what they see** – this may be to point out an animal with a younger child or about the different actions of a character with an older child. When a response is offered the following interactions provide support:
  - **affirming what the child has said** – '*Yes they are going to sleep*';
  - **substituting an appropriate response**: '*You think the duck makes a "ribbit" sound, do you? Well, I think you are teasing me because I think a duck says "quack"*';
  - **extending the child's response by adding information:** '*Yes, that's right, chimpanzees are bigger than monkeys but monkeys can't walk on two legs like chimpanzees!*' In this type of interaction the adult supports the child's learning, whilst maintaining the child's self-confidence.
- **Sustained interactions** – as children's understanding grows the adult might extend the child's thinking in sustained interactions which include some of the above including: **commenting, describing, conjecturing, questioning, scaffolding thinking and providing different perspectives or opinions**.

Practice review C&L 3: Speaking

The focus of Speaking at the end of the EYFS is set out in the Early Learning Goal (ELG) for this aspect, which is '*children express themselves effectively, showing awareness of listeners' needs. They use past, present and future forms accurately when talking about events that have happened or are to happen in the future. They develop their own narratives and explanations by connecting ideas or events*' (DfE, 2012: 8). In order to arrive at this point children need many experiences of social communication which allow them to engage with others sometimes listening and sometimes speaking in order to express their ideas, thoughts and feelings. Encouraging every child to be a skilful communicator involves capitalising on every opportunity as well as creating contexts which encourage children's talk.

Everyday practice

Consider the pedagogical responses below:

Daniel who is 2 years 4 months, is playing alongside three children in the outdoor area. With the help of an adult the children have built a helter-skelter for balls using a series of drain pipes balanced on crates. As each ball rolls through Daniel is more and more excited – running off to the nearby ball pool shouting '*I det more*' he comes back carrying three blue balls in his hands and says '*I dot loads*'.

a) As Daniel arrives back with the balls in his arms the practitioner moves sideways to allow him to get into position to roll the balls. As he pushes the first one down – she says: '*That was great, Daniel, it went really fast!*' When the balls run out again she says: '*Oh oh! We need some more now!*'

b) The practitioner says: '*You have got loads now – what colour are they, Daniel?*' Daniel looks uncomfortable for a moment thinks for a while and says: '*Red*'. The practitioner smiles and says laughingly: '*No, they're not red; they're blue like the sky! You know that, Daniel!*'

c) The practitioner says: '*You have got quite a lot, let's check.*' She then points to each ball saying, '*One, two, three*'. She then pauses for a moment to give Daniel time to listen again saying '*You've got one, two. . . . .*' and Daniel says '*Three*'. '*Yes, Daniel*' she replies '*you've got three balls*'. She then says '*I've spotted something else about the balls you have chosen, what do you think I have noticed?*' Daniel looks at her and then says in reply: '*I dot loads*'. The practitioner responds: '*Yes, and the ones you have chosen this time are all the same colour – like the sky – they're all blue! Are you going to roll them down the pipe to see if they fall into the box at the end?*' She waits and Daniel says '*Yes*' and begins again rolling the balls.

Questioning everyday practice

Daniel's learning characteristics:

> Daniel is very keen to get the extra balls to continue the game – an example of *'Showing curiosity about objects'* (DfE/EE, 2012: 6) which is one of the characteristics of effective learning: Playing and Exploring. He is also determined and motivated, aspects of Active Learning.

Pedagogical response review

In (a), the reactive response, the practitioner's focus is on the game which she appears to be enthusiastic about. Whilst she has connected with Daniel by commenting on his actions she has missed opportunities for encouraging him to be the speaker. In (b), the partial response, Daniel's words have been affirmed by the practitioner but his understanding of the meaning of the word 'loads' has not been expanded or clarified. By omitting to explore his conceptual understanding of 'loads' the practitioner has missed an opportunity to widen Daniel's vocabulary. The practitioner did not re-present or re-cast the word 'got' (Daniel pronounces this 'dot'), which might have subtly alerted Daniel to the correct sound at the start of the word. Focusing on a discussion of the colour of the balls has restricted a more open-ended discussion, though new vocabulary was introduced to the child and it was obvious his remarks were recognised as conveying a message. In (c), the extended response, the practitioner offered a substitute for 'loads' by suggesting that the child had 'quite a lot', which was then clarified when the adult pointed to each ball saying, 'one, two, three'. Giving Daniel time to think and scaffolding his response by saying: 'You've got . . . . .' before Daniel said 'three' was a way of helping him to feel successful. The adult's open-ended comment: 'I notice something else about the balls you have chosen', allowed Daniel to be right whatever response he gave – so that when he repeated: 'I dot loads' the practitioner was able to extend his vocabulary and move on to encourage him to continue with the game leaving Daniel's efforts at speaking rewarded. To support his learning further pedagogy could focus on building his language and maintaining his motivation to notice patterns – this might involve developing a collection of objects for Daniel to explore.

Consistently giving children time to formulate their thoughts and then to speak is a necessary investment of time which encourages children to progress from the use of words and gestures to more complex speech patterns enabling them to become skilful communicators.

Effective practice: Experiences that support speaking

- **Conversation partners** – babies and young children need conversation partners who take every opportunity to support their talk and communication. These are based on first hand experiences which create a genuine context for discussion; one-to-one time and being in small groups allows more talk time for individuals.
- **The right word at the right time** – sensitive practitioners provide key words the child needs, emphasising relevant words and phrases. The practitioner might support the child in an exchange with their parents asking – *'Are you going to tell daddy about George's **dinosaur**?'*
- **Signs, non-verbal communication and symbols** – communication does not, consist of words alone since it involves cognitive and physical development as well as social skills. Some children will communicate through signs and visual symbols as well as non-verbal means, for example: *'Makaton uses speech with signs (gestures) and symbols (pictures) to help people communicate. . . . . also use facial expression, eye contact and body language to give as much information as possible'* (Makaton website, 2013). Learning to communicate meaning is supported and facilitated by the quality and sensitivity of adult interaction with the child.

Quality interaction

Quality interaction with sensitive adults provides:

- **A role model for language** – through **naming, labelling and describing** items
- **Sustained shared thinking** by focusing on cause and effect, explanations and considering questions such as 'What if?'
- Encouragement to **explain or suggest reasons for things happening** – Practitioner: *Why did the red hen not want to share the bread with the pig I wonder?*
  Child: *No, no!*
  Practitioner: *That's right; the pig said 'No', when he was asked to help. I think that the hen was cross with the pig, what do you think?*
- Support for children's understanding of **past, present and future events in time** – *'You are **going** to Jack's birthday party **tomorrow**, that's exciting?'* Or, *'**Did you have fun** at Milo's house **yesterday**?'* or *'**I love** carrots – I think they are the best part of my lunch **today**'*.
- Understanding that **language is a tool for making meaning** enables children to formulate and express their thoughts, then modify and amend their ideas in the light of new information.

PHYSICAL DEVELOPMENT (PD)

The first three years of life take the infant from dependence on others to relative autonomy physically, their reflex actions reducing in concert with the development of intentional movements which emerge as the child achieves hand-eye coordination, dexterity and large and fine motor control. Natural though all this may look it relies on the child's motivation to reach out to others and on their receiving encouragement from those around them. Research on otherwise healthy children left for more than six months in Romanian orphanages where there was low emotional warmth and interaction, found that in spite of there being care such as feeding and changing, children *were likely to have abnormal brain development (small brain), abnormal EEGs and low metabolic activity. They were also more likely to display autistic behaviours, ADHD, aggression, antisocial behaviour and poor cognitive development at age 11'* (McCain *et al.*, 2011: 44). This and other similar findings emphasise the importance of individual and continuous care by as few people as possible for children up to the age of three in out of home settings. In a discussion of ways to support physical growth and development in young children a family science specialist at North Dakota State University (NDSU) identifies three areas of focus for parents to facilitate their young child's skills: gross motor, fine motor and balance and co-ordination skills, reminding that patterns of physical development *may vary based on a child's age, physical maturity and developmental context'* (such as the presence of developmental delays)' (Brotherson 2009: 1).

For babies, skills such as lifting and turning the head, raising the head and holding the head steady appear to be simple yet take time to develop, and arise from having opportunities to extend and retract the spine and to move position. As children gain control in this way other skills such as stretching and kicking also develop; these skills help the child to move in correspondence to the strength of the spine and muscles, leading eventually to the child sitting for short periods, creeping and crawling before walking independently.

Even when a young child has begun walking the system for balance can be unreliable and the young child is often unable to stop and hold a movement. As the toddler gains greater control the ability to coordinate hands and eyes in action leads to play which extends skills such as bending and lifting in order to reach an item, pushing a truck or propelling a push-along toy.

Play with different sized balls encourages throwing, catching, rolling and kicking and often includes skills such as running and chasing. Balancing is difficult for a young child and takes time to perfect since the weight of the upper body is disproportionate to that of the lower body. Supporting children to try simple activities such as sitting on a log, or walking along a plank, can help to develop balance; crawling through and over objects will support function of the vestibular system, important in balance. Jumping also relies on balance and progresses from approximations such as putting one foot in front of the other and moving forward with effort, to jumping on the spot and then to jumping a short distance forwards initially – then backwards as children gain greater control and precision in movements of this kind.

Many of the large motor skills that the young child achieves are frequently developed through everyday activities in the home or the setting and through play – these might include – climbing on and off furniture, rough and tumble play, adjusting walking to match the surface – for example on sand or a slope; galloping, moving to music and stopping and starting. Similarly, fine control also arises from handling items, for example, manipulating or manoeuvring items such as a car, a xylophone beater or a spoon. PD is central to all other development and is considered in relation to the following aspects:

- Moving and Handling
- Health and Self-Care

Practice review PD1: Moving and Handling

The focus of Moving and Handling at the end of the EYFS is set out in the Early Learning Goal for this aspect, which is *'children show good control and co-ordination in large and small movements. They move confidently in a range of ways, safely negotiating space. They handle equipment and tools effectively, including pencils for writing'* (DfE, 2012: 8). This begins as the child has experiences which helps them gain control over their own body through having opportunities to stretch, reach, grasp, move, turn and roll in the first months of life. This leads literally to an expansion of their horizons as they become mobile and exploratory through developing the skills of crawling, standing, walking and climbing. This aspect is also about the child becoming adept at playing with items such as pushing a ball, hitting a rattle, or squeezing a toy to make a sound. One- and two-year-olds will also pull and push things to move them toward or away from them. Using scissors, crayons, felt pens and paint brushes become achievable as children's small motor movements are refined when with increased access they begin to use a range of tools and equipment.

Everyday practice

Consider the pedagogical responses below:

> Roisin, who is within weeks of her third birthday, tells everyone she is a 'football man' – and she tries to play football cheering loudly when a 'goal' is scored, and since there is no obvious goal post she enjoys scoring lots of goals.
>
> a) The practitioner goes along with her behaviour enjoying the cheering and recognising that Roisin is getting a good deal of physical exercise as well as pleasure from her activity.
>
> b) The practitioner considers that Roisin might benefit from playing with several others who are also interested in football. He introduces the idea by reading a story focused on 'favourite things', which Roisin enjoys. Roisin then is encouraged to demonstrate how she can kick an imaginary ball. Paving the way for taking forward this idea the practitioner suggests that the next day Roisin might like to wear a special football strip.
>
> c) The practitioner has been aware that whilst this activity is giving Roisin lots of exercise and fun there is little development from it so he takes Roisin to look at a football pitch and then gives her a book showing girls as well as boys playing football. He shows the little girl how a goal is scored and plans with her how to set up a goal area; helping her think what it should be made of and where it will go. He also helps her to make a scrap book about football, adding stickers and pictures from magazines.

Questioning everyday practice

Roisin's learning characteristics:

> Roisin is motivated and keen to play; she maintains focus and shows high levels of energy and fascination in her chosen interest: football. These are examples of Active Learning (DfE, 2012: 7) as is her pride in scoring goals.

Pedagogical response review

In (a), the reactive response, the practitioner simply accepts that Roisin is getting exercise and having fun and is very supportive of this; he does not seem to question Roisin's view that she is a 'football man', thinking this is an amusing way of describing herself as a 'footballer'. In (b), the partial response, the practitioner has considered ways to involve Roisin's interest in a more 'organised' way since he thinks of introducing her to a game with others. He has also identified that wearing a special football strip might extend Roisin's interest in a slightly different direction. In (c), the extended response, the practitioner has reflected on the amount of time the child spends in this pursuit and has used Roisin's interest to help her understand what scoring a goal involves. Additionally, he has supported her to consider ways to create a realistic goal area. The practitioner has also focused on broadening the child's explorations through introducing her to the idea of making a scrap book, connecting aspects of literacy as well as extending her view of who can play football, by helping her to recognise that footballers can be female as well as male.

Skills connected with throwing, catching, kicking and handling balls are excellent for hand-eye coordination as well as balance and locomotion. Focusing on these areas also supports wider cognitive and physical outcomes.

Effective practice: Experiences that support Moving and Handling

- **Frequent movement** including crawling, rolling, walking, jumping, running and balancing. Young children should always have lots of opportunities to move about since sitting still is almost impossible for the very youngest children.
- **Tummy time** – for the youngest children floor play on the tummy as well as on the back; encouragement to roll over, or creep towards toys just out of reach;
- **Soft play** – for older babies and toddlers soft play and access to surfaces at different levels with slight slopes or low steps as well as to a range of equipment that supports standing, walking, climbing, kicking, jumping and running.
- **Action games** – simply squeezing a soft toy or wiggling fingers supports the child's fine motor skills which are essential for activities such as self-feeding with a spoon or mark-making with a felt pen.

- **Access to a range of resources** – children who are given lots of time to experiment will, with support, develop the confidence and skills to become efficient tool-users.

Practice review PD2: Health and Self-Care

The focus of Health and Self-Care at the end of the EYFS is set out in the Early Learning (ELG) for this aspect, which is that *'children know the importance for good health of physical exercise, and a healthy diet, and talk about ways to keep healthy and safe. They manage their own basic hygiene and personal needs successfully, including dressing and going to the toilet independently'* (DfE, 2012: 8). With younger children Health and Self-Care focuses on how children learn about practices that will keep them healthy and safe – these might include understanding that if something is 'hot' it mustn't be touched – even at twelve months babies begin to respond to such messages. During this period adults also help them understand how to handle food with clean hands and not to eat things that have fallen on to the floor and to understand why some foods are health promoting. Another element of this aspect is independence in self-care – which at first glance appears surprising, particularly with the youngest babies, however young children do become aware of expectations in a social group and often want to show off their skills by feeding themselves, choosing to use a toilet rather than a potty, partially or wholly dressing or undressing themselves and attempting to wash their own hands.

Everyday practice

Consider the pedagogical responses below:

Eighteen-month-old Josh is new to the setting and seems reluctant to try to feed himself with a spoon. Having discussed this issue with his parents it has been established that Josh's family have found it preferable that he didn't make a 'mess' and older siblings have fed him, and now whilst he has the physical skills he seems uninterested in feeding himself. After this discussion it has been agreed that the setting will work with the family to encourage Josh to feel pride in his own achievements so that he is motivated to try feeding himself. After a few days as lunch time approaches Josh is seen in the home corner sitting on a settee next to a doll which he is carefully feeding with a spoon, from a bowl of 'food'.

a) The practitioner says to him: '*Wow Josh, are you feeding her yourself? Clever boy! It's nearly time for your dinner now – are you going to feed yourself like you're feeding the dolly?*' and soon after s/he asks him to finish off because it's time to '*wash our hands and go for lunch*'.

b) The practitioner sees this as a 'break-through' and takes the opportunity of Josh's complete involvement in feeding the doll to use an iPod to take a video of Josh to replay later so s/he can share it with his family.

c) The practitioner observes how carefully Josh lifts the spoon to the doll's mouth and his concentration as he waits while the doll 'eats' the pretend food. S/he comments on what he is doing saying: '*Josh is feeding the little baby. Josh is putting some food on the spoon for the baby and Josh is giving the baby her food.*' As the practitioner comments on his actions Josh continues to carefully feed the doll finally putting the spoon down and saying '*All gone*'. S/he then turns to Josh and says: '*Can dolly come to have lunch with us and perhaps Josh can show her how to eat her dinner?*' Josh smiles and the practitioner invites him to bring the doll, spoon and bowl to the table for lunch where s/he sets a special place next to Josh for the doll, suggesting to Josh that he try a 'spoonful' of dinner first, before feeding a spoonful to the doll.

Questioning everyday practice

Josh's learning characteristics:

Josh demonstrates aspects of the characteristic of effective learning: Playing and exploring. This is evident in the way he engages in the new experience of feeding the doll, learning by trial and error and playing with what he knows. He will benefit from being encouraged to be proud of his own accomplishments, an aspect of Active Learning.

Pedagogical response review

In (a), the reactive response, the practitioner was aware of Josh's achievement in feeding the doll independently and knew that the strategy the setting had devised was working, since Josh was clearly interested in and successful at feeding the doll. However, s/he praised Josh for being clever, rather than for his efforts at feeding the doll and rather than capitalising on his obvious interest s/he ended his involvement by asking him to stop for lunch. In (b), the partial response, the practitioner is mindful of the significance of the event seeing it as a 'break-through' but his/her involvement is focused on how s/he will use what she has learned about the child to support him in the future – the video offering evidence to share Josh's achievements with his parents. In (c), the extended response it was clear that the practitioner recognised that in transition many things seem overwhelming. S/he recognised that this might be affecting Josh as well as the fact that he is fed at home by older siblings. S/he therefore used the opportunity presented when s/he saw Josh engaging in the actions normally done by his older siblings, to appeal to Josh's capable self, rather than the 'baby' self he had adopted. S/he then seized the opportunity to extend the feeding of the doll into the lunch session by providing a place beside Josh at the table for the doll.

When babies and young children are given opportunities to try things – whether that is to try to feed themselves or to climb on to a chair independently, they experience feelings of competence which nurture their feelings of autonomy and self-confidence.

Effective practice: Experiences that Support Health and Self-Care

- **Supporting independence** – this can seem difficult at times, particularly if adults are hurrying to meet deadlines – home time, lunch time, nap time and so on, yet investing time to support children's independence pays dividends in terms of children's emotional well-being as well as their independence.
- **Flexible schedules and routines** – allowing sufficient time for children to develop skills encourages children to test out their ideas and find out what they can do. Occasionally deviating from a routine should not be too disruptive for most children if there is a predictable structure most of the time.
- **Offering a variety of foods** – children learn to try new foods and broaden their tolerance of new tastes.
- **Commenting positively** – on how children follow the rules that keep them safe. If this occurs when tidying away, for example, the child learns about ways to prevent or avoid hazards.
- **Paying attention to their own needs** by discussing with children if they are hot or cold, hungry or thirsty helps them to recognise how they are feeling and to identify ways to keep healthy.

This area of learning is closely linked to children's personal, social and emotional development, the focus of the following section.

PERSONAL, SOCIAL AND EMOTIONAL DEVELOPMENT (PSED)

Personal, social and emotional development is arguably the foundation of all other learning since it centres on the child's attitudes to themselves and others and to events, experiences and activities as well as their beliefs about their own ability and about learning itself. Research shows that children who believe they can succeed are more likely to achieve, a self-belief which is key to success. Based on the work of Carol Dweck, a psychologist, 'mind sets' are described as either 'growth' oriented or 'fixed', explained in this way: *'people tend to have two extremes of belief about themselves, that are the key to their effectiveness or ineffectiveness. One extreme is of a self that is an **unchanging entity** and the other extreme is of **a self that is constantly changing** in varying increments. Dweck asserts that one theory is highly adaptive for the human condition (the theory of an incremental changing self) while the other is maladaptive for the human condition (the theory of a self that is an unchanging entity)'* (Learning Knowledge website, 2013). The theory suggests encouraging children to recognise this by practising or trying skills such as taking photos with a camera, or manipulating a paintbrush will help them to get better at the skill, which affirms them in a growth mindset: *'I achieved it because I tried'*. Whilst merely valuing achievement encourages the child towards a fixed mindset – *'I did it because I was good at it'*. This suggests that when adults interact with children they should comment positively on the child's efforts: *'I noticed you tried really hard when you put your hood on, then you pushed your arms into your sleeves – that was a really good effort. Now I'll help you to pull up your zip. I know you'll soon be doing this all by yourself – because you are good at trying!'* Dweck refers to this approach as process, rather than outcome praise.

Babies' and young children's feelings are rarely hidden and because their brains are still developing they do not have the ability to manage their feelings – these skills are learned through experiencing reassurance from adults. In order to manage their feelings and subsequently their responses to life events it is now accepted that babies and young children need to develop skills known as executive functions, defined as: *'the capacity to manage what we attend to and think about, and how we combine this new information with what we already know'* (Whittington, 2012: 4). These skills include: working memory, inhibitory control, and cognitive or mental flexibility (Centre on the Developing Child:Harvard University, 2011: 2). Why are these skills considered important to learning in the early years? They are seen as important because they form the building blocks of self-control – so, for example developing working memory helps children in social interactions with others – for example to take turns in a group, to join in with a group, or to re-tell a story. Whilst inhibitory control acts like an inbuilt monitor for inhibiting unwanted or unacceptable behaviour – so it prevents the child from hitting out at others, snatching or becoming distracted by peripheral events. Cognitive or mental flexibility '*is what enables us to apply different rules in different settings*' (ibid.: 2) and is the skill which helps the child to know about expectations of behaviour in different settings, distinguishing what is acceptable for them to do at home compared with what might be recognised as acceptable in the setting. This means that whilst there is flexibility in routines there should also be some predictability and pattern to the day and children should be supported to understand the pattern through clues such as visual timetables which can be discussed with them; music which signals quiet times, or tidying up or sleep time; provision of familiar and new songs, rhymes and stories and warm recognition of wanted behaviour and consistent handling of unwanted behaviour. Developing these capacities continues beyond early childhood but children who develop them successfully are described as able to '*focus on a number of pieces of information at one time, sort out what to take notice of and what not, to work out when they have made a mistake and make decisions based on what they know. They do not act impulsively, but rather consider all they know about a situation before they act*' (Whittington, 2012: 6).

In her discussion of the importance of social–emotional development for learning, Adele Diamond, Professor of Psychiatry at the University of British Columbia asks '*What do we want for our children?*' responding by saying '*We want our children to grow up good human beings*' and proposing that to foster that outcome there are two things we can do: '*One is to be a role model of that ourselves*' and the other is to recognise that '*children learn what they live*'. In other words, she argues '*If we want more kind and considerate children, we need to give them kind and considerate role models, and we need to give children boundless opportunities to practise kindness and to experience for themselves how making someone else happy makes them happy*' (Diamond, 2010: 789). This approach leads children towards reciprocating acts of kindness and helps them become caring to others and sensitive to others' feelings. However it does not happen automatically and only occurs if it is facilitated by caring adults who model the desired behaviour. PSED does not, of course, occur in isolation from other areas of development but links to them, affects them and is affected by development in them.

PSED is made up of three aspects:

- Self-confidence and self-awareness
- Managing feelings and behaviour
- Making relationships

Practice review PSED 1: Self-confidence and Self-awareness

The focus of Self-confidence and Self-awareness at the end of the EYFS is set out in the Early Learning (ELG) for this aspect, which is that *'children are confident to try new activities, and say why they like some activities more than others. They are confident to speak in a familiar group, will talk about their ideas, and will choose the resources they need for their chosen activities. They say when they do or don't need help'* (DfES, 2012: 8). Arriving at this point is a process which begins with children experiencing unconditional love and positive regard in their earliest attachment relationships with parents, siblings and other family members. These provide the child with a secure base from which to develop independence not only physically but also emotionally. Nurturing relationships support the child's self-confidence and lead the child to an acceptance of themselves regardless of their individual abilities and attributes and to a respect for themselves and others.

Everyday practice

Consider the pedagogical responses below:

Thirty-four month old Logan always chooses the 'big' bike when he is outside telling his key person: *'I'm a big boy, I'm a big boy, I'm the biggest!'* He tends to prefer his own company and sometimes gets into arguments with other children because he pushes them away telling them they can't play because they're not big.

a) The practitioner is aware that Logan lacks confidence and that he uses a limited range of resources but believes that he should be allowed to make choices. So, she leaves him to play independently a lot of the time, reducing his 'turns' on the bike by giving him little jobs to do indoors as he also enjoys helping. When he is outside on the bike she extends his experiences by getting him to set up road layouts such as a crossing with small traffic cones to manoeuvre round.

b) The practitioner decides to focus on finding ways to enhance Logan's self-esteem by encouraging him to show the younger children how to do things such as how to tidy away carefully or how to serve drinks or snacks and other little jobs. As part of her support for this area she adds a special section to his Learning Journey to show the things he is good at.

c) The practitioner is aware that Logan lacks confidence and that he uses a limited range of resources but believes that he should be allowed to make choices so she introduces a timer on the setting's iPod – this can run for any length of time and emits a loud alarm when the time is up. She encourages Logan to use the timer to check how long it takes him to complete little challenges, some with the bike and others without it, such as completing an obstacle course, running a 'marathon', finding five hidden objects to claim a prize and so on. She finds that he is successful at these and then encourages him to show other children what to do which he enjoys. She praises him for the way he helps the others to look at the numbers on the iPod, to ride the bike and for carefully looking for clues on the treasure hunt. She avoids praising him, or the other children for being fastest or best.

Questioning everyday practice

Logan's learning characteristics:

> Logan shows particular interests – an aspect of Playing and Exploring. He is also able to maintain focus on an activity for a period of time and he persists, aspects of Active Learning.

Pedagogical response review

In (a), the reactive response, the practitioner shows she has thought about Logan's needs to some degree, recognising she should reduce his 'turns' on the bike by giving him other experiences. She has also extended the resources to use with the bike, though she has not found ways to increase his self-esteem, nor to encourage him to get along with his peers. In (b), the partial response, the practitioner recognises that Logan's self-esteem will not develop without considerable support from herself and others. She therefore sees her approach as one which will pay off longer term. Developing Logan's learning journey together with Logan and his parents might also increase his self-esteem. In (c), the extended response, the practitioner has recognised that the environment is not offering Logan the challenges he needs. Her reflection on her own practice leads her to consider ways to support him to engage in Active Learning and to develop self-confidence since she is aware that his claiming to be the 'biggest' indicates his self-esteem might need support. She is also aware that older two year olds are often ready for new challenges and diverting their interests from being the 'best' can help them to develop self-confidence and to recognise that positive feelings and satisfaction can derive from different sources, such as helping others.

Effective practice: Experiences that support Self-confidence and Self-awareness

Ways to help children become self-confident include:

- offering praise and recognition for effort, rather than achievement;
- finding things that the child enjoys that illustrate their unique orientation to the world – for example celebrating the fact that a child knows lots of things about clouds, or motorbikes or loves a particular type of music;
- talking about the things they can do;
- talking about the things they are learning to do;
- sharing photographs of children with their families and discussing why they are special in their family and what makes their family special;
- celebrating birthdays, special days or small events in a child's life such as becoming a 'big sister' or 'big brother', learning to use a potty, or to blow into a tissue;
- making books that focus on 'ways we care for ourselves' and 'ways we care for one another'.

It is important to use process praise, commenting positively on what the child is doing well, so that the child feels pleased with their efforts, rather than only their achievements.

Practice review PSED 2: Managing Feelings and Behaviour

The focus of Managing Feelings and Behaviour at the end of the EYFS is set out in the Early Learning (ELG) for this aspect, which is that *'children talk about how they and others show feelings, talk about their own and others' behaviour, and its consequences, and know that some behaviour is unacceptable. They work as part of a group or class, and understand and follow the rules. They adjust their behaviour to different situations, and take changes of routine in their stride'* (DfE, 2012: 8). The processes supporting children's development in this aspect spring from warm, generous and supportive relationships provided by significant people in their lives, such as parents, siblings, grandparents, the key person and their substitute in a setting and other influential adults. This area is especially important in reducing children's chances of experiencing mental health problems, since it promotes children's sense of well-being.

Everyday practice

Consider the pedagogical responses below:

Twelve-month-old Harriet screams and throws herself back because she can't get her favourite doll out of Hameed's arms.

a) The practitioner rushes over to the two children and says to Harriet *'No!'* as he lifts Hameed into his arms. *'You can't have it now, Harriet'* he says kindly – *'its Hameed's turn – you can get it later'*. He then allows Hameed to continue holding the doll, while Harriet sobs loudly.

b) The practitioner rescues the situation helping the two children to calm down then suggests that Harriet would like to play with a teddy which is in a basket nearby.

c) The practitioner quickly intervenes to ensure Hameed is unhurt then gently puts his arms around both children saying: *'Oh dear Harriet, are you really, really cross, because you can't have the doll? Are you very sad?'* Then, turning to Hameed who looks unperturbed he says: *'Are you alright, Hameed, was that a bit of a shock? I think it probably was! I think Harriet is cross, aren't you, Harriet.'* After a moment or so he says: *'Harriet, would you like to be friends with Hameed when you have calmed down and you are feeling better?'* Harriet is still crying hard so the practitioner says: *'Shall we show you how to get another doll to play with from the cot so that you and Hameed can both play with a doll? Do you think that's a good idea?'*

Questioning everyday practice

Hameed and Harriet's learning characteristics:

Hameed and Harriet are both *'showing curiosity about objects'* (DfE/EE, 2012: 6) which is one of the characteristics of effective learning: Playing and Exploring.

Pedagogical response review

In (a), the reactive response which Harriet received it was clear that the practitioner felt it was necessary for young children to learn to share. This is part of the process of developing social skills; however babies and very young children do not have the necessary understanding of the effects or consequences of their actions, nor is it possible initially for them to share toys and equipment without support. In (b), the partial response the practitioner is interested in conflict resolution rather than problem-solving and has omitted to offer either children support to manage their feelings or behaviour. In (c), the considered response, the practitioner has recognised that Harriet's feelings are intense and that in order to manage them she needs help. He has therefore checked that Hameed is unhurt and acknowledged Harriet's feelings. His decision to help Harriet to choose an identical doll from the cot in order to prevent the incident recurring shows he understands children's development and is therefore redirecting Harriet's behaviour.

'Redirection means that when a child acts inappropriately (doing something not wanted by others), staff help the child focus on something else to do that is appropriate to achieve his or her goal' (Cryer et al., 2004: 357). Opportunities for learning about sharing could also be provided through experiences such as looking at books together, or listening to music in a small group.

Effective practice: Experiences that support Managing Feelings and Behaviour

- **Key Person and one-to-one time** – children are helped to manage their emotions best when adults help them to feel safe and secure so their experiences are positive. Offering reassurance and support when they are upset or distressed through providing narratives and commenting on their feelings helps them to solve problems through considering alternatives.
- **Developing simple rules and strategies to support the expression of feelings** – children make sense of their experiences through observing how 'rules' are applied and they develop hypotheses based on their understandings of what to do where, and how to behave in certain situations. When rules are consistently applied children quickly become adept at adjusting to expectations; when this is not the case children become confused and uncertain about what is expected. Therefore rules should be few, simple to understand and easy to apply.

- **Commenting positively when children apply a successful feelings or behaviour management strategy.** For example: '*I noticed you stroked the rabbit very gently*', or '*That was kind when you comforted Billy when he was upset after his mummy left*'.
- **Displays and books focused** on feelings give children opportunities to think about their own feelings, recognise that other children share similar feelings and to discover ways to resolve or deal with feelings, including knowing to turn to trusted adults for help.
- **Creating independent access to resources** – babies can be given access to resources which are within reach so that they can make choices – this might include proximity to mirrors, floor-level displays of family photographs or favourite characters from stories.

Practice review PSED 3: Making Relationships

The focus of Making Relationships at the end of the EYFS is set out in the Early Learning (ELG) for this aspect, which is that '*children play co-operatively, taking turns with others. They take account of one another's ideas about how to organise their activity. They show sensitivity to others' needs and feelings, and form positive relationships with adults and other children*' (DfE, 2012: 8). Young children base their understanding of how relationships work on the relationships they experience in the home and in the setting. They assume that all relationships work in the same way until they are mature enough to re-appraise these. These set the context for how they behave and how they treat others and are significant in how they learn to function in later life.

Everyday practice

Consider the pedagogical responses below:

Five-month-old Emilia and six-month-old Albie are placed alongside each other on a soft blanket; their key person is close by. The two babies have been placed side by side to encourage their communication with one another and both seem to enjoy the short period when this happens, and whilst Emilia doesn't look at Albie for most of the time, she does vocalise when Albie is near.

a) The Key Person watches the babies for a short time then turns away briefly from time to time do some writing. She occasionally makes eye contact with one or other of the babies but after a short while gets up saying '*It's time for your lunch, now*'.

b) The Key Person joins in with Emilia or Albie in conversation. She also comments on Albie's movements – saying in a playful tone: '*Are you rolling over again? You're so good at getting about now; soon there'll be no stopping you!*' This type of interaction seems to maintain the babies' involvement for about 10 minutes or more.

c) The Key Person watches each baby's interaction and says to Emilia: '*You're talking to Albie aren't you, what are you telling him, I wonder? Were you saying to him "You're my friend"?*' She then smiles and gently strokes Emilia's cheek. Next she looks at Albie who has rolled on to his tummy and who is vocalising loudly in Emilia's direction – she says to him '*You have got a lot to tell your friend, haven't you Albie, are you telling her its fun being together?*' She pauses so that Albie has time to respond, vocalising more. Then she says '*Are you two going to play together when you get older? I think you are!*' She takes a photograph of the babies and later puts a copy of the picture in each child's file and on a friendship display.

Questioning everyday practice

Albie and Emilia's characteristics of learning:

Both babies show they can maintain focus on their activity for a period of time – this is an example of Active Learning since they are both involved and concentrating. Albie is also curious about people (Emilia) since he spends time looking at her and vocalising in her presence – this is an example of a child finding out and exploring.

Pedagogical response review

In (a), the reactive response, whilst the babies have been brought to the same spot to be together the Key Person has attached little importance to the encounter and clearly has not considered ways of supporting their relationship. In (b), the partial response, the practitioner is supporting the babies' engagement in communicating. She is also positive and playful and may consider that simply placing the babies next to one another is a way to support them in making relationships. In (c) the considered response, the practitioner has recognised that the babies are communicating and because she has spent time observing them she is mediating the experience for both babies by scaffolding the encounter, suggesting what one baby might be saying to the other. By encouraging both babies to communicate she is supporting them to build the fundamental skills of making relationships through being with one another, and finding pleasure in being part of a social group.

Babies enter the world ready to relate to others and the responses they receive shape the interactional style they develop. However the benefits of acquiring social skills are high, and the lack of them is undesirable since it has been shown that *'our thinking and our brains suffer if we are lonely or feeling socially isolated'* (Diamond, 2010: 783), hence the importance of children learning how to get along with others.

Effective practice: Experiences that support Making Relationships

- **Greeting and departing routines** – welcoming each child by name and when they leave telling them they will be missed by their friends.
- **Focus on friendship** – encouraging children to recognise the characteristics of friendship helps them to distinguish their own good points and to discuss why they like certain children.
- **Circle time** – provides a context for discussion of cooperative ideas such as sharing and taking turns – these are though, difficult concepts for young children to understand or abide by in the early years.
- **Story** – listening to stories helps children work out which characters they prefer and how to show kindness to others and deal with unwanted behaviours.
- **Display photographs of families and people children know** – discussing the characteristics and attributes of others gives children positive role models to aspire to.

A final note in relation to pedagogy with children from birth to three is that its apparent simplicity belies its complexity.

7 Teaching and learning in the Prime Areas: From three to five

Whilst many good reasons exist for continuing the same approach to teaching and learning as is followed in respect to younger children, as children mature expectations of them change in line with their development and differences in approaches to teaching and learning become observable.

Whatever approach is taken it will be important to consider children's different levels of development, rather than their chronological ages. A further consideration is that the curriculum should be developed in light of the EYFS requirement: '*Each area of learning and development must be implemented through **planned, purposeful play** and through **a mix of adult-led and child-initiated activity**'* (DfE, 2012: 6). This statement appears clear, however, since expectations at the end of the EYFS are expressed as Early Learning Goals (ELGs) there is a risk that teaching children in reception and nursery age groups could become overly focused on these outcomes leading to an imposed (Mantle of the Expert website, 2013), rather than an emerging curriculum. Clearly, there is a balance to be struck here about how to support children to achieve the prescribed EYFSP outcomes through a play based approach which must derive, according to guidance in the revised Early Years Foundation Stage Handbook from: '*Responsible pedagogy* [which] *must be in place so that the provision enables each child to demonstrate their learning and development fully*' (STA, 2012: 9). Therefore professional discussions must underpin decisions relating to approaches to pedagogy with three to five year olds. This is especially important in the case of single reception classes in schools where a top down approach might influence requirements about planning as well as approaches to teaching and learning. So is effective pedagogy in the Prime Areas distinctive in any way, when children are three, four or five years old, or is this the same as for younger children?

How does everyday practice support children's learning (aged 3–5 years) in the Prime Areas?

Just as with babies and young children up to two years of age, establishing relationships with them, as well as with their parents, is a priority. Cordial relationships are important at all times, and are particularly significant when a child has specific needs which require support at home and in a setting, whether that is a school or pre-school. Including all children is a requirement in the EYFS and by the time a child reaches their third birthday information from the Two Year Progress Check should be available to any new setting from a previous one (or room, if the child has moved within a pre-school). This, together with any other records should inform discussions with parents about the child's development in the Prime Areas of Personal, Social and Emotional Development, Communication and Language, and Physical Development.

All young children spend a great deal more time at home with family members than they spend in an out-of-home setting. As a result, by the time they enter the last two years of the EYFS they bring with them many different feelings and experiences from home – such as being listened to, being loved and cared for, watching TV, sharing a joke, using a language, vocabulary and grammar based on what is the norm in their own environment and with this they bring a sense of self derived from these experiences. They also store experiences from attending other settings or of being members of different 'rooms' in the same setting. Whatever their experience is, children will have learned a great deal about negotiating at least two complex environments and relationships within them. They will also have absorbed unwritten 'rules' within the two environments (this may be more) and there is the potential their learning journey may be fragmented when they move between different 'stages of the EYFS', brought about by their transfer between different environments. Another concern at this time is the move from pre-school to reception class when a step change in expectations often occurs because children have entered the 'school phase'. Therefore a priority for these four and five year olds is to ensure that radical changes in expectations and in pedagogical style do not occur to dent children's self-confidence.

Making connections

Taking account of what has been discussed previously it is helpful to consider how children make connections in their learning as they mature. These connections have been conceptualised, by one theorist as: neurological, cognitive, social and experiential (Cross, 1999: 7). The first of these, is now understood to be highly significant, since it is known *'sensory stimulation strengthens* [neural] *connections, while connections . . . that are seldom or never used are eliminated*' (ibid.: 7), highlighting the importance of, for example, a dual language learner using their home language in addition to the language they are learning in the setting.

Cognition or coming to know about the world is also seen as a series of connections, often revealed by young children's schemas or cognitive structures that '*consist of facts, ideas and associations organised into a meaningful system of relationships*' (ibid.: 8). Through playing, exploring and active learning and being engaged with adults in sustained shared thinking children develop their own ideas and understanding – for example, the four year old who asks for a drink of water on a wintery day when snow is lying on the ground may, in discussions with an adult, encounter the idea that the water is colder than usual because the underground pipes that run to the setting are buried under the ground – this is a potential trigger for a child's scientific skills and deductive thinking, which at a later stage will lead to deeper learning. Notably learning theory stresses the significance of it being easier '*to learn something where we already have some background than it is to learn something completely new and unfamiliar*' (ibid.: 9).

Arguing that '*learning and a sense of identity are inseparable*' (Lave and Wenger, 1991: 115) since they are both aspects of the same phenomena, learning researchers, Lave and Wenger illustrate perfectly a theme of this book: that is the significance of the social aspects of learning, or the context in which learning takes place. Very young children are as much co-constructors of their learning as are older students – since they bring with them their own 'theories', and make considerable efforts to try to make sense of the world (Donaldson, 1978), however complicated this may seem – until concepts such as 'getting in a line' (that is invisible) or 'making an effort' (from something you can't see) have some meaning for them. So pedagogy, whilst intended to help young children to learn, can sometimes be a source of confusion and recognising this is important. The final approach through which children make connections in their learning is *experiential*. This term is most readily recognised in early childhood education in relation to the work of Ferré Laevers, who focuses on the relationship between the child's emotional well-being and their level of involvement. This suggests that when this is optimal children '*feel at ease, act spontaneously, show vitality and self-confidence*' and are '*concentrated and focused, interested and fascinated*' since they are acting '*at the very limits of their capabilities*' (Laevers, 2011: 1). Experiential learning is generally understood, to emanate from David Kolb's work and the words, of Confucius: '*Tell me, and I will forget. Show me, and I may remember. Involve me, and I will understand* (Greenaway, 2013). This is the 'learning by doing' model recognised by early years educators from the time of John Locke in the seventeenth century (Elkind, 2012) to present day proponents of the 'plan, do, review' model found in High Scope and similar approaches.

Whilst all the elements of 'connection', neurological, cognitive, social and experiential, may occur, these processes are largely invisible; the challenge is to find the contexts which allow the child to be engaged and to want to learn. Dewey warned: *'Perhaps the greatest of all pedagogical fallacies is the notion that [a] person learns only the particular thing he is studying at the time. Collateral learning in the way of formation of enduring attitudes, of likes and dislikes, may be and often is much more important than the . . . lesson . . . that is learned. For these attitudes are fundamentally what count in the future. The most important attitude that can be formed is that of desire to go on learning'* (Dewey/ Hall-Quest, undated). Children's motivation to learn can be supported through providing pursuits and contexts that have meaning for them.

In common with the EYFS, early years curricular usually focus on contexts such as play as a vehicle for learning, alongside other approaches including direct teaching, modelling and adult-guided activities as well as those which are led by children.

The guidelines referred to earlier helpfully suggest *'five main contexts for learning and development'* that *'teachers purposefully create'*, these include:

- *'Play*
- *Real-life situations*
- *Investigations*
- *Routines and transitions*
- *Focused learning and teaching.'* (Queensland Studies Authority, 2006: 32)

Whilst play, routines and transitions and focused learning and teaching are self-explanatory and will not be discussed in depth here, it is useful to define 'real-life situations' and 'investigations' which are explained in the following ways: real-life situations are those which take into account and draw on social and cultural diversity, enabling children to make connections between home and classroom and might include cooking, gardening, reading and writing text for real purpose, conducting an experiment, or talking with visitors about their roles (ibid.). These are very similar to the activities and experiences offered by many EYFS settings. Investigations are described as arising from *'the questions children ask, from ideas and events that arouse their curiosity or from the need to collect further information for something they might want to do'* including *'comparing the mass of everyday objects; exploring how sound is created using vibration, using books and communication technologies to investigate a topic of interest, creating maps and diagrams to communicate ideas, investigating ways to use art materials and processes, creating patterns with real objects, testing out ideas about ways to move their bodies or other objects'* (ibid.: 35–36).

Each of the different approaches listed above is seen to offer a different route into the curriculum and provides a perspective on how an early years curriculum can be developed in line with the principles of the EYFS to achieve the Early Learning Goals at the end of the period.

Contexts for learning (3–5s)

Because three to five year olds have a wider experience than babies and toddlers, contexts for learning also widen somewhat though still include most of those discussed in relation to younger children. Now, however, children are often more likely to discuss their experiences, or bring to the setting items from home such as a picture, or a book and may have particular agendas such as wanting to discuss their favourite activity or TV programme (watched before coming to the setting). Alternatively they may be intrigued by materials the practitioner has prepared or be excited and curious about the prospect of using a new resource or of helping develop an area in the learning environment. These provocations are described as '*learning invitations*' by Kathryn Delany, a project facilitator with the Educational Leadership Project in New Zealand. Delany suggests that '*An expansive learning environment is full of provocations . . . that foreground being disposed to learning in positive and expansive ways*' (Delaney, 2011: 3). Going on to explain that expansive learning environments '*strengthen, broaden and enrich the learning related dispositions of those who participate in them*' (ibid.: 3), Delany is referencing the approach in Reggio Emilia, Italy, where the environment for learning is described as the 'third teacher'. This links well with the EYFS principle of the enabling environment, therefore a significant factor, besides developing links with parents, is the nature of the environment and how it is presented to children, which should be borne in mind throughout this chapter.

Provocations for learning

With children from three to five years many opportunities for developing young children's learning arise – the key to supporting children's interests is to plan for possible lines of development in children's learning and to have a wide range of resources ready for when a child's line of enquiry emerges. These might relate to those discussed in the previous chapter, in addition to any or all of the following:

- **'Finds'** (Investigations) – children often develop a passing interest in something they have 'found' either at home or in the setting – 'finds' might include natural items such as acorns, leaves or an old bird's nest; or items that are unusual such as foreign coins. 'Finds' might need a 'home' so a child might make a 'leaf box' or they may become part of imaginative play – the coins becoming pirate's treasure – to be integrated into play and added to.

- **Extending an experience** (Real-life situations) – a trip to a pantomime, for example, may be enjoyed by all children, but the event might inspire some children to set up and create the theatre, complete with torn up paper for tickets and chairs set out in rows, with an impromptu performance of singing or dancing. This type of trigger for exploration might be inspired by any number of things including a bus ride, a visit from a safety officer or attending a football match

- **Shows based on stories** – (Play and Real-life situations) slightly different from the above – children will sometimes be inspired to present shows because of particular props or enhancements – for example reception children celebrating Divali were observed using scarves, sarongs and masks to re-live the story of Rama and Sita, opening the show with the words: 'Ladies and Gentlemen I present to you . . .'.

- **Pretend play** – (Play) young children often play complex games of pretence and the characters they take on can be as varied as animals, fairies, princesses and 'baddies' depending on what has inspired the play.

- **Puppets** – (Focused teaching and learning and Play) quiet children can often relate to puppets because they appear non-threatening and often less 'knowledgeable' than the child (if an adult is the puppeteer). When the child is in charge of the puppet they often reveal different behaviours from normal – such as becoming strong – by being the wolf, rather than Red Riding Hood, or acting in role as one of the three little pigs who is afraid of the big bad wolf.

- **A TV programme** (Investigations) seen at home – young children are often intrigued by programmes they have watched and can be knowledgeable about the words to jingles such as 'Thomas the Tank Engine', 'Charlie and Lola', '64 Zoo Lane' and many others. Television is not always viewed as an educational tool yet children may be interested and intrigued by ideas that they encounter at home, and with support they might wish to find out more about them or follow up in the setting.

- **Obstacle course** (Investigations) – children are often inspired to set up areas which look like obstacle courses made up, indoors, of cushions, soft play blocks and mats and outside incorporating crates, sacks, planks and tunnels – interactions should encourage children to consider ideas such as risk and safety, ways of moving and mounting and dismounting.

- **Large construction as pretend play** – (Play) the creation of alternative worlds through the use of large items and the availability of large hollow blocks, willow dens, weather cubes, staging and

lattice panels can provide structural outlines which together with the provision of interesting materials such as canvas, netting and camouflage can support the creation of imaginary worlds.
• **Exploration of contrasts** – (Investigations and Focused teaching and learning). Exploring can interest children in investigating differences in contrasts such as high, low; black, white; up, down and so on.

How such different provocations support children's learning as well as teacher-led activities are the focus of the next section which considers pedagogy in the Prime Areas with three to five year olds.

In the practice reviews that follow, short examples of child/adult interaction are set out in relation to each of the Prime Areas. Each vignette provides an example of teaching and learning opportunities which typically occur in settings catering for three to five year olds; the intention in offering these examples is to highlight the nature of what pedagogy looks like in practice with young children and to offer pause for reflection about both its nature and significance. The sections, which follow each vignette are intended to offer a lens for reflection on:

• Everyday Practice
• Questioning Everyday Practice
• Effective Practice

These are offered as examples to facilitate reflection on pedagogical responses and the discussions that transform children's learning and development. Possible responses are considered in relation to each vignette – none of the responses is proposed as being correct or incorrect – they are simply examples of the types of responses observed in different settings over a period of years. These are presented as:

• (a) reactive responses – which may occur when attention to the aspect of learning has not been thoughtfully considered
• (b) considered responses – which occur when opportunities are taken to capitalise on significant aspects of learning

Their purpose is to prompt discussions about the nature of pedagogy, and about how relationships support the child in their sense of being understood and valued, an entitlement for every child in the EYFS. Following each short case study the characteristics of learning are briefly considered in relation to each child as well as different provocations for learning.

Unlike the previous chapter, where each aspect of the Prime Areas was considered separately, in the following three sections each of these areas of learning is considered holistically, beginning with Communication and Language.

COMMUNICATION AND LANGUAGE

A continuing concern with four year olds at school entry has been the number of children presenting with speech, language and communication difficulties; though the majority of difficulties are transient. The evidence distinguishes between those children with Speech, Language and Communication Needs (SLCN) who '*may have problems with production or comprehension of spoken language, with using or processing speech sounds, or with understanding and using language in social contexts*' (Hartshorne, 2009: 3), children who are likely to have long term, persistent difficulties compared with those with impoverished language who with the right support may catch up with their peers. The latter group, whose speech and language skills are found to be immature or poorly developed, have '*speech* [which] *may be unclear, vocabulary* [which] *is smaller,* [and their] *sentences are shorter and they are able to understand only simple instructions*' (ibid.: 3). The difficulties of this group are considered to be mainly transient difficulties which can be overcome with appropriate support, however an issue for practice is that in some areas there may be a prevalence of children with such difficulties since '*in some parts of the UK, particularly in areas of social disadvantage, upwards of 50% of children are starting school with speech, language and communication needs (SLCN)*' (ibid.: 3).

Distinguishing between speech, language and communication is important if children's needs in this area are to be met. The following descriptions from the Communication Trust are helpful in this regard:

> **Speech refers to:**
> - *Speaking with a clear voice, in a way that makes speech interesting and meaningful*
> - *Speaking without hesitating too much or without repeating words or sounds*
> - *Being able to make sounds like 'k' and 't' clearly so people can understand what you say*
>
> **Language refers to talking and understanding:**
> - *Joining words together into sentences, stories and conversations*
> - *Knowing and choosing the right words to explain what you mean*
> - *Making sense of what people say*

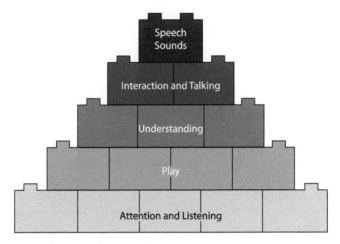

Figure 7.1 Communication development pyramid

Adapted from a model used in many speech and language therapy services across the UK. Reproduced with kind permission from The Communication Trust.

Communication refers to how we interact with others:
- *Using language or gestures in different ways, for example to have a conversation or to give someone directions*
- *Being able to consider other people's point of view*
- *Using and understanding body language and facial expressions, such as:*
  - *knowing when someone is bored*
  - *being able to listen to and look at people when having a conversation*
  - *knowing how to take turns and to listen as well as talk*
  - *knowing how close to stand next to someone'*

(The Communication Trust, 2011: 7).

The way this is achieved through the gradual development of speech, language and communication in communicative supportive environments, is summed up in Figure 7.1 (ibid.: 9).

Another report indicates: '*A communication-supportive environment at pre-school and the primary school will enhance a child's language at this crucial developmental stage and minimise the effects of transient communication difficulties*' (Hartshorne *et al.*, 2011: 12). Therefore the environment and the nature and quality of interaction influence communication. A toolkit for focusing on communication provides a checklist which suggests that a communication friendly environment is one where:

- there are not too many visual distractions;
- unnecessary noise is eliminated;
- pictorial information is offered and labelling and displays support children's understanding; *together with there being*
- clarity about routines and expectations.

A further message is that ways of interacting with children are based on practitioners' knowledge of language development and their provision of strategies to support children's communications, including children being able to say when they don't understand (Communication Trust, 2010). Practical suggestions to support this approach are based on quality first teaching which is successful with all children, including those with SLCN. The TALK technique (ICAN, 2008: 1) outlines the following approaches:

- **Listen more than you talk** – and give children time to talk before you interject;
- **Involve children in conversations** – ensuring that you use simple language and that there is a balance between adult and child contributions;
- **Use visual cues** so that young children with SLCN needs are able to communicate their responses to choices on offer (and in the process reduce their levels of frustration);
- **Emphasise turn-taking** in conversation as well as activities;
- **Value what children say** – by listening to them attentively and sensitively (this enhances self-esteem);
- **Look at the child**;
- **Say their name**;
- After giving instructions **check understanding**;
- **Reinforce and extend a child's language** development by commenting on what is happening, providing them with a model to support their own language and repeating language that a child is learning.

It is clear that in promoting the speech, language and communication development of three to five year olds there are many issues – most of which are beyond the scope of this publication, however the following categories from Talking Point (ICAN, 2011) are helpful in thinking about provision across five broad areas of language development, which whilst not symmetrical with the aspects of C&L in the EYFS are closely aligned with these and could be considered in any planning for this area with three to five year olds (Table 7.1). These have been presented to consider the role of the practitioner as well as the contexts where these may occur in relation to C&L:

Table 7.1 SLCN across five broad categories

Type of Talk	Context	Interaction
Attention, Listening and Understanding Concerned with knowing to look at the person talking, and being aware of what is being said; listening to instructions without needing to look up; understanding instructions comprising two or three parts and answering 'how' and 'why' questions.	Small group sessions focused on rhymes, poems and play with sounds, through games such as I Spy or adding new words to known rhymes and tongue twisters. Routines, for example during a review of what groups of children have been doing, or plan to do. This might include feedback from role play by 'the three bears' and children may comment on what they found when they looked at their porridge bowls, or their chair or when they discovered Goldilocks.	Modelling and encouraging children to be aware of the importance of listening to a speaker; telling children that although you might not be looking at them (perhaps whilst helping a child to push their foot into a shoe), you are still listening. Giving positive feedback to a child who listens and carefully follows instructions comprising several parts.
Vocabulary Understanding a range of words to describe concepts such as rough, smooth, cold, hot; knowing words can be put into categories such as animals, or flowers, or toys and being able to clarify to make meaning clearer – 'it was a dark and misty night'.	Story time when a small or larger group share books and opportunities for discussion arise naturally. Sorting for a real purpose where classifying is necessary – for example: all the big crayons, felt pens, pencils are stored beside one another and collections of objects are separated for the next user. New words are introduced in relation to everyday events – the weather, climbing, jumping and so on.	Re-presenting what children have said with the addition of new words; Introducing new words in discussion with children – for example, 'I think that hat fits baby bear perfectly' or 'Yes, that is a lovely tree, it's an evergreen; evergreens don't lose their leaves in Winter'.

(Continued)

Table 7.1 (*Continued*)

Type of Talk	Context	Interaction
Speech Sounds, Grammar and Sentence Building Using well-constructed sentences, which are mainly clear and correct – though difficult words such as 'spaghetti' may be shortened; joining phrases with conjunctives such as 'and', 'so', 'because'.	Explaining why a particular method was used to achieve an end such as why they decided to fix a mask with transparent tape because a 'transformer's mask' needed to be 'see-through'. Re-telling a story or talking about an event that is important to them such as how they got ready to go out after a heavy snow fall.	Scaffolding the child's efforts by: giving sufficient time to allow them to think about what they want to say; offering comments or questions that might support them – for example, 'That sounds just like what I did too, I got my wellingtons out and my hat just like you did – and I got something else too, did you?'
Verbal Storytelling and Narrative This is an area focused on retelling events with detail, as well as retelling favourite stories – using some of the words in the story as well as their own words and describing events, though not always joined together or in order.	Resources such as iPads, iPods and easi-speak devices and similar items encourage children to listen to and retell stories and parts of stories to then share with a group. Role play often supports narrative particularly if props to support recall of the story are available.	Modelling and extending children's thinking through using a story frame approach and commenting on the separate parts of the story to help children understand that these can be identified as the 'beginning', 'middle' and 'end'.

| **Conversations and Social Interaction**

Here the child is engaged in joining in or starting up conversations with other children, joining in with role play alongside other children and pretending to be somebody else; talking as well as using language for a range of purposes including asking questions, negotiating and giving and discussing opinions. | Circle time is an opportunity for children who feel ready and able to talk aloud to do so in a very supportive environment; songs, stories and rhymes which encourage children to take on roles are also useful – for example different groups could make the animal sounds or be the narrator in stories such as *What the Ladybird Heard* (Donaldson, 2010).

The use of 'talk partners' also familiarises children with the idea of the importance of discussion; plenaries and 'interviewing' as part of 'hot seating' also encourage children to ask questions. | Modelling the importance of listening carefully to others; 'thinking aloud' – for example, 'I think I'd like to know more about how the robbers in the story got past the dog.'

Asking children to explain how they succeeded in doing something such as – achieving an award for swimming, finding a 'lost' puzzle piece or building a 'boat' from crates. |

Practice review: Communication and Language

Everyday practice

Consider the pedagogical responses below:

A four year old, Sasha, has chosen to paint a picture in the EAD area. Using yellow paint to begin with, to create a blob, she then surrounds this by a larger, circular image, to which she adds radiating lines commenting '*That's the sun*'. She then creates another yellow 'blob' lower down the paper and then quickly adds blue paint saying '*I'm mixing the paint – its turned green, look it's turned green!*' quickly turning with excitement to tell the adult nearby, as a patch of khaki-green paint appears. In a moment another large red blob of paint is created which she says is '*United*' because '*it's red*'. She continues to paint and there emerges yet another red circle opposite to the red blob which after several paint strokes resembles a figure with eyes, nose, mouth, legs and arms – there is movement in the picture.

a) The practitioner welcomes Sasha, when she first enters the art area, reminding her to put on an apron and to write her name on the paper so that she will recognise her painting at 'home time'. Whilst Sasha is painting he busies himself with helping another child into an apron and writing the child's name on his picture, nodding pleasantly when Sasha expresses her excitement at the sight of the blue and yellow paint turning green. He looks at the picture which Sasha is painting saying – '*Is United your favourite team?*' to which the child replies '*Yes*'. The practitioner praises Sasha telling her: '*I love your picture, you've used yellow for the sun, red for the ball and the man and green for the grass, well done!*' He suggests that at another time the girl could try to paint the person's eyes in a colour such as 'blue' or 'brown' and then tells her to put the painting on the rack to dry, reminding her to wash her hands since she has finished painting.

b) The practitioner is interested in observing the 'story' behind Sasha's picture and notes that the picture is made almost entirely of circles and straight lines. He comments to Sasha that in her picture he can see four different circular shapes – and that some of the circles are 'filled in' (the blobs), whilst others are not (the yellow sun). Sasha tells the practitioner she loves going round and round with her brush and her favourite part of the picture is the green that she has mixed. The practitioner asks Sasha to tell him about her painting which Sasha does, affirming that her favourite part is the green section. In response the practitioner likens the shade of green to the camouflage netting which has been used to make a den in the garden. This leads to a discussion of camouflage in animals. When she finishes the practitioner asks if Sasha will allow him to hang the painting on the wall when it is dry so that everybody can see her picture and Sasha agrees, leaving the area to find the story of *The Mixed-up Chameleon* (Carle, 1988), a story about animals which is based on the idea of why it is important to be confident about who you are. A short time later she asks the practitioner: '*Have you hanged it up yet?*' And the practitioner replies: '*No, I haven't hung it up yet but I will shortly, as soon as it is dry. While we are waiting it would be a good idea if you could write your name on a label to put next to your picture, so that people will know you are the artist who painted it, would you like to do that for me?*'

Questioning everyday practice

Sasha's learning characteristics:

> Sasha is beginning to demonstrate some aspects of each of the characteristics of effective learning. She is maintaining focus on the activity, and shows high levels of fascination, this is illustrative of Active Learning; she is also playing and exploring since she has the confidence to explore colour in the way she chooses and is demonstrating her innate curiosity; she is also willing to take a risk by mixing the colours straight on to the paper so is creating and thinking critically.

Provocation for learning:

> This is an example of a real-life situation in which the child is connecting what she knows from her life at home with her experiences in school or the setting. As much as this scenario describes the child's exploration of colour and form it also sheds light on the child as a communicator and a learner.

Pedagogical response review

In (a), the reactive response, the practitioner has provided Sasha with several opportunities to talk and listen, to follow instructions and to answer a question. He has also provided Sasha with a period of uninterrupted time in which to explore colours and to create a picture of her own choosing. In (b), the considered response, the practitioner has been involved in significant discussion about what interests Sasha most about her picture: the creation of a new colour, green. This has led to discussions comparing the shade of green with the camouflage netting (making connections from what is known), to discussions about the chameleon who changes colour to become part of the background in any situation compared with having the self-confidence to be 'who he is'. Finally the interaction has provided new vocabulary, an opportunity for genuine discussion, and has offered Sasha a model of the grammatical structure she has attempted to use with reference to 'hanging' the painting.

Planning time for encouraging the development of sustained, meaningful discussions may need consideration of ways to reduce managerial discussions (perhaps substituting spoken instructions with written and oral messages, on discs, for example) in order to increase time focused on supporting children's speaking and listening skills, including ways to clarify children's understanding in different contexts.

> **Effective practice: Experiences which support communication and language with three to five year olds**

This list should be read in conjunction with the suggested experiences in Chapter 6.

- **Adults speaking less and listening more** in small group times. ICAN, the children's communication charity states: *'It is easy when working with young children to talk most of the time; giving information, asking questions and directing'* (ICAN, 2008: 1). Giving status to children's talk reduces this.
- **Providing effective role models of language** which allow the child to understand why the adult is doing a particular thing – for example, 'I was thinking that we could have put the sunshades up outside today because it was so sunny but now that all those clouds have appeared I'm not sure, what do you think?'
- **Encouraging children to talk** about what they have been doing (or finding out) about in the setting and giving them the time to think about it, explore their ideas and tell others.
- **Allocating children partners for talking** – so that in a one-to-one situation each child is developing the skills of leading a discussion. This ensures that when children are asked for feedback from discussions, they are more confident because they have rehearsed what they want to say, which promotes their willingness to speak aloud.
- **Providing mirrors, dressing up clothes**, microphones, karaoke machines, stages and recording devices that encourage children to try out a new persona or a big voice in a non-threatening situation.
- **Facilitating discussions** about favourite and least liked parts of stories, or plays and encouraging all children to participate.
- **Playing games** (either commercial or devised for particular groups of children) that encourage listening, stopping, and thinking and following one or more instructions – these might include: playing statues or imitating another child such as in 'Simon Says'.
- **Story telling** – where a story is explored and illustrations are discussed. This might lead to predicting what will happen next or to recounts using props.

PHYSICAL DEVELOPMENT

Recent government statistics show that in a National Child Measurement survey with high participation rates *'In Reception, over a fifth (22.6%) of the children measured were either overweight or obese'*. And, as previously, there was *'a strong positive relationship . . . between deprivation and obesity prevalence for children in . . .* [this] *age group. The obesity prevalence among Reception year children attending schools in areas in the least deprived decile was 6.8% compared with 12.3% among those attending schools in areas in the most deprived decile'* (DoH, 2012: 7).

Taken at face value these figures are startling, however the bigger picture reveals that by Year 6 one in three of children (22.6%) were overweight or obese and the percentage of obese children in this group (19.2%) was double that of reception year children (9.5%) in 2010/11. These figures suggest that establishing good habits in the early years is essential if children are to be supported to make wise choices about lifestyle. This is developed through Physical Development in the EYFS with its two aspects: Moving and Handling and Health and Self-Care.

Opportunities for physical development linked to play are of the utmost importance including: large-motor play, small-motor play and rough and tumble play (Miller and Almon, 2009), since habits such as exercising and taking part in physical activities are established early. Understanding children's need for large-scale and vigorous play is important since some adults who do not understand its significance can find such play disturbing and purposeless. Therefore leaders should ensure that all those working with the youngest children recognise that through their play children develop many physical skills including fine and gross motor skills as well as balance, movement and agility – they also learn about the effects of exercise on the body and ways to care for themselves – including making healthy choices such as resting or drinking water after exercising. Further opportunities are provided in many settings, especially schools, for Physical Education (PE) where large indoor and outdoor spaces offer a range of equipment such as mats for tumbling and stretching, planks for balancing and climbing and benches for travelling or traversing, amongst other things. Additionally large spaces are also often available for moving and making music – which also involve many physical challenges including being still, listening to sounds and patterns in music and moving when certain sounds are heard. The following skills can be developed over time in contexts that support safe exploration and children receive support to reflect on their actions:

Table 7.2 The development of physical skills

Type of Skills	Context	Interaction
Control and co-ordination in large movements. Move confidently in a range of ways Control in large movements is the first task of the young child. This proceeds in a cephalocaudal direction; that is, from the head to the lower body. Children develop these skills through standing, balancing, walking, running, jumping, climbing, rolling, galloping.	Moving between rooms or different areas in a setting. Playing in a large space – such as out of doors; in a hall, a swimming pool or the park. During specific exercises or activities attended outside of school or setting or in addition such as football practice, gymnastics, swimming lessons, dance classes, cycling and so on. Holding and manipulating a parachute in a group; riding a bike; trampolining. Painting with large brushes big spaces.	Talking about ways of moving – 'do you think the woodcutter ran or walked to Red Riding Hood's grandma's house?' Providing language to describe movements: 'slowly', 'quickly', 'heavily' and 'lightly'. Planning what movements children might use if they were trying to walk soundlessly: tiptoeing Discussing how children move in different situations – for example how they push their legs to propel a swing forward. Discuss the importance for good health of physical exercise.
Control and co-ordination in small movements. Handle equipment and tools effectively. Know the importance for good health of physical exercise, and a healthy diet and talk about ways to keep healthy and safe. Manage their own basic hygiene and personal needs successfully	Dressing and undressing: Hanging up coats; putting on and pulling off shoes and socks; pulling zippers. Self-care: using a hanky or toilet paper, putting soap on hands, rubbing hands with soap and rinsing fingers. Eating: opening food wrappings, holding and eating finger foods; undoing drink tops; holding a straw in place in a drink.	Talk about ways to handle equipment and tools safely 'I notice you are holding the scissors correctly – the handles are pointing outwards – that's safer'. Model and talk about a comfortable grip with a writing implement. Encourage children to discuss their choice of lunch, or if they bring lunch talk about their favourite healthy items in their lunch box.

Fine motor control results from proximodistal development, which moves outwards from the centre of the body to fingers and toes at the extremes. The child gains control of arms before hands and of legs before toes. Children develop these skills through grasping, pushing, pulling, holding, twisting, turning and lifting small objects and coordinating the movement of the hand with what they can see – through hand-eye coordination.	Using small items such as farm animals; threading beads; turning pages in a book; pointing to words and pictures. Exploring the properties of malleable materials such as dough or clay; making marks in glitter or sand. Fixing and making items using hammer, nails or glue, tape or staples. Playing with cars, dolls, magnets and other items. Using a magnifying glass, or feeding a rabbit. Making marks using a stylus, fine paint brush, pencil or felt pen.	Create displays which illustrate a healthy diet and encourage children to map their preferences on it by putting their picture or name card near the foods they enjoy. Model ways to keep healthy and safe, such as washing hands in the toilet area, keeping areas clean and free from hazards. Encourage children to manage their own basic hygiene and personal needs successfully, by praising beginners who try to pull up a zip, or put a coat on independently – plan with the child next steps to achieve dressing and going to the toilet independently.

Practice review: Physical Development (ages 3–5)

Everyday practice

Consider the pedagogical responses below:

Three-year-old Qasim is a quiet little boy who loves looking at books about animals and says his favourite pastime is watching TV at home. He is taking part in an adult-led activity intended to support development of fine and large motor skills through creating sounds and moving to music. Qasim is very interested in the activity and watches intently; the practitioner inviting him to choose an animal from the bag – which he does, pulling out an elephant. Qasim is delighted that he has selected the elephant because it is his favourite animal – and, because he has taken part in the activity previously he jumps up tripping slightly, but ready to move like an elephant. As soon as the children begin to beat and shake their instruments to create a loud rhythmic noise he moves forward, holding his arm in front of his face like an elephant's trunk, slowly lifting his feet off the ground he slowly swings forward, then sideways. He succeeds in moving to the music though he has trouble stopping when the music stops but at the end all the children clap – at which he looks very pleased. On his next turn, when he is balancing on one leg, like the grey geese he has pulled from the bag, Qasim struggles to keep his balance.

a) The practitioner notes that Qasim's physical skills are within the expected range for a child aged between 30 and 50 months but decides to observe him more carefully and encourage him to take part in a greater range of physical activities to extend his skills. She also decides that she will differentiate her planning for the next session so that children move for the whole time instead of sitting playing the instruments because she has noticed that some of the children are not as interested in playing the instruments as in pretending to be the different animals.

b) The practitioner notes what Qasim is able to do well – he is keen to join in activities; he is able to select animals from the bag, he is aware of how an elephant lumbers along with big plodding steps and he can listen to the music and start moving when the music starts. However, she is concerned that Qasim struggles to stand on one leg for a very short period and is aware that he is not as confident physically as other children of his age. She goes back to his pre-school record and finding no reference to any issues with motor control she decides she will have a discussion with Qasim's father when he collects him from school. This is because she is concerned that he stumbled and had difficulties in balancing and she has gathered from discussions with Qasim that when he is at home watching TV he stands right up to the screen, where he tells her 'You can see better'. She decides to ask his father's opinion if he thinks Qasim's eyesight should be checked.

Questioning everyday practice

Qasim's learning characteristics:

Physically Qasim has many capabilities and is evidently a child who uses what he knows in his play, uses his imagination and is willing to 'have a go' – all aspects of the characteristic of effective learning: Playing and Exploring.

Provocation for learning:

This is an example of a focused learning and teaching session. The practitioner is sensitive to Qasim and has planned an activity linked with his interests, which allows him to display what he knows about animals such as an elephant.

Pedagogical response review

In (a), the reactive response, the practitioner has used *Development Matters* to guide her judgements about Qasim's physical skills and has also recognised the importance of encouraging him to engage more in physical activities – these are both important points to have considered, she has additionally evaluated the session she was leading, deducing that it was not appropriately meeting the needs of the whole group. In (b), the extended response, the practitioner has considered Qasim's development holistically taking into account transition information as well as her own observations and because she has talked to him about what he enjoys doing at home she is aware where he positions himself whilst watching TV. She has concluded that since his coordination was not previously an issue the cause may be more recent and possibly connected with his sight.

Supporting children's Physical Development is about providing children with a range of opportunities not only to develop their physical skills but also to consider how to keep themselves healthy and safe. Physical skills are being refined all the time well beyond the period of the EYFS. Supporting a child's development in a particular area may involve working with parents to ensure that a child is receiving the same 'messages' at home as at a setting – for example, what is a 'safe' distance to watch the TV from. Vigilance about potential or actual difficulties with eyesight (and hearing) can prevent long term damage if noticed and dealt with early enough.

> *Early childhood is the optimal time to teach and learn fundamental movement skills. During this period young children are motivated and keen to master ways of moving, controlling their bodies and coordinating their movements*
>
> (CCEA, 2006: 2)

Effective practice: Experiences that support Physical Development (ages 3–5)

In addition to all the resources children engage with daily such as sand, water, small world, construction and many more the following activities support this area.

- **Say and Do activities** (Focused teaching and learning) might include games focusing on – walking in different directions, for example: forwards, sideways, backwards; tip-toeing; running and stopping at a signal; running on the spot; jumping on the spot and over a short distance; walking along a plank up to 18 centimetres from the ground; crawling through a tyre, over a bench (University of Minnesota, undated).
- **Ball games** (Focused teaching and learning and Play) – throwing, catching, kicking, rolling, batting, aiming, goal scoring – using makeshift posts; throwing into a target such as a net or a bucket.
- **Music and dance** (Focused teaching and learning, Investigations, Real-life situations and Play) – body percussion – clapping,

stamping, banging fists; using percussion instruments such as shakers, clackers, poppers, barrels, cans, pans; routines – 'elephant walks like this . . .'.

- **Outdoor activities** (Focused teaching and learning, Investigations, Real-life situations and Play) (many also take place indoors but some may only happen outside) – den building, gardening, caring for animals, mud kitchens, collecting natural items, stepping stones, climbing wall; fetching and carrying water, sand, mud and stones; painting, chalking on a large scale; block play; dance rings, maypole; sitting and rocking bowls, rope walks; parachute; wheeled toys: trucks, bikes, carts, wheelbarrows; capes, superhero play.
- **Small World** (Play and Investigations) Miniature worlds require careful handling of small items – these might include a dolls' house, garage, underwater scenario, woodland creatures, farm animals and other small items.
- **Interactive displays** (Routines and transitions) – 'What is for lunch today?'; healthy snack display; hand washing routine display; spot the difference display – safety; ways to take care of myself display – drink water; take exercise, eat healthy food, have a good night's sleep, rest when I'm tired.

PERSONAL, SOCIAL AND EMOTIONAL DEVELOPMENT

As indicated in the previous chapter, Personal, Social and Emotional Development is an area of considerable concern and interest throughout the life span, and there is now increasing recognition of the importance of this area of development for children's long term mental health since it is recognised that early experiences can either support or compromise a child's sense of self, self-worth and self-confidence.

Routines

Optimum development in this area derives from a child feeling a sense of safety and security which is built up over time as they learn to trust those adults who are responsible for their care. When these needs are met their attention can be focused on learning; when these needs are not met they may be distracted and distractible and unable to engage with others. It is known that *Once children reach the preschool and early years of school they can manage their thinking and how they act much better than previously, but still depend on close adults for guidance*' (Whittington, 2012: 3). It is important therefore to ensure that routines and transitions are established so that there is a predictable pattern to the day which helps children to identify what comes next as well as to understand which part of the day has gone and what is still to come, particularly important because at the beginning of this period children are rarely able to tell the time or accurately judge different lengths of time.

Predictable events in the day for a three to five year old might be: arrival and registration, free-flow time, gathering of Key Person groups (depending on the space and numbers of practitioners available at particular times), focused teaching times, lunch time, story times and home time. However, flexibility and individual approaches to the timings which occur will be different for every setting.

The most important aspect of this is how these give a shape to the child's day allowing them to feel confident as they arrive, are greeted and become relaxed in the setting, and moving from one person's care to another's (the care of a lunch-time supervisor), and from indoors to outside and so on. This is because rules, expectations and interactions are likely to alter from one situation to another and comprehending these can be problematic if children are not supported to know what is appropriate behaviour in each situation. If these considerations are addressed it is likely that children will make progress in their learning because discontinuities will be reduced to the minimum. This will give opportunities for them to develop positive relationships with other children and with adults; to develop confidence in trying out activities and in choosing resources and to develop independence through being aware of boundaries and expectations in the variety of contexts in which they spend significant amounts of time.

In order to make relationships with others, develop self-confidence and self-awareness and to successfully manage their feelings and behaviour young children need the support and feedback of caring adults who model the desired behaviour and provide contexts for practising emerging skills. Skills of relating to others occur as children play alongside and with other children, gain entry into play, lead play and share their ideas because these experiences help them to understand the reciprocal nature of relationships and their own contribution to group dynamics.

Ultimately this approach leads them to get along with others, and to develop an understanding of how to recognise and avoid potential points of conflict through a problem-solving approach. Self-understanding and self-acceptance underpin the child's development of self-awareness and self-confidence both of which stem from experiences which support the child's sense of identity within the dimensions of similarity and difference. Identifying shared characteristics helps children develop a sense of belonging in the setting, supporting them to act on their own initiative, to be resourceful and to feel confident to make choices.

The sense of belonging to a group is positive yet must be experienced within an understanding of difference and diversity – in other words, group membership should offer a secure base from which the child is able to explore the differences between themselves and others, as well as to identify and celebrate the ways in which they are similar to others. This approach leads children to recognise that difference is inclusive since it extends to all individuals, families and communities, none of which is considered superior, or valued more than another.

Another major task for the young child relates to their capacity to understand and manage their feelings and behaviour. Again young children's abilities will reflect many aspects of the ways adults model behaviour in situations which are stressful, energising or problematic. Therefore a strategy should be in place which supports children in identifying and labelling their feelings and reflecting on ways they and others respond to them. This could occur through both incidental and planned discussions and through explorations of stories and real-life events in which feelings and behaviours are considered. Through this approach children begin to draw conclusions about the effects of their own and other's actions and to understand that cooperation with others is more effective than conflict. Californian State guidelines provide excellent advice in relation to promoting this area in preschools and schools, suggesting that to: *'successfully support social-emotional development, the curriculum must be designed to:*

- *allow many opportunities for practising social interaction and relationship skills;*
- *provide support for the growth of age- and developmentally appropriate self-regulation abilities;*
- *encourage curiosity and initiative; and*
- *provide each child a network of nurturing, dependable adults who will actively support and scaffold his or her learning in a group setting'* (California Department of Education, 2010: 40).

The following table (7.3) identifies some of the skills, attitudes, approaches and opportunities to support children's development in PSED:

Table 7.3 Skills, attitudes, approaches and opportunities to support PSED development

Skills and Attitudes	Context	Interaction
Making relationships Relating to others through being kind and friendly to them.	Children learn desirable skills and attitudes from adult role models and from older children.	Discuss with children what it feels like when somebody is kind; friendly or cooperative.
Being aware of own needs and sensitive to others' needs.	Circle time or small group times are useful for talking about needs and preferences such as why somebody likes to sit in a particular place – so they can see clearly or to be alone for a short time.	Comment positively on children's smallest efforts to recognise their own and others' feelings.
Playing along with others.	Caring for a pet, cultivating plants and tidying can offer opportunities for children to cooperate with others or to take on a responsibility.	Discuss motives and behaviours of story book characters or superheroes identifying the impact of different types of actions.
Cooperating with others to achieve a shared outcome.		Seek children's views about how to resolve issues – so that they develop the ability to see that there is more than one solution – for example play can involve more than two children – three can play together if everybody cooperates.
Recognising differences can be resolved and compromising to reach a favourable solution.	Well-chosen stories can be a good source of discussion focused on dilemmas about behaviour or about emotions.	

Self-confidence and self-awareness		
Recognising and understanding own feelings.	*'Use the family culture to create bridges between the program and the home, supporting children's pride in their family experience, and understand individual differences in background and viewpoint'* (California Dept Education, 2010: 42).	Share stories about the child's life at home.
Recognising and acknowledging that sometimes others have different feelings from mine.	Plenary sessions provide opportunities for evaluating whether something was difficult or easy for different children.	Take every opportunity to celebrate children's efforts as well as their achievements. Help children to feel confident to speak about their community or religious or cultural events.
Trusting myself to make good choices.	Ebooks or paper versions of books that tell 'Our story' – for example: 'In this class we speak 17 different languages; We know about these countries; We like to eat these foods and so on; The things we can do'.	Celebrate festivals that are meaningful to children – discuss the music associated with different events – for example joyful or solemn.
Being proud of my own efforts.		
Being pleased when others are successful.	Displays – which reflect similarities differences, achievements and efforts.	
Knowing we are all different, with different abilities and yet recognising we are all equally valued.		

(Continued)

Table 7.3 (Continued)

Skills and Attitudes	Context	Interaction
Managing feelings and behaviour Tuning in to my own needs. Understanding my own needs.	Feelings occur in almost every context and opportunities for identifying, labelling and talking about feelings arise across the day – however Key Group sessions lend themselves to exploring feelings – such as 'I was happy when . . .'; 'I enjoyed . . .'; I like to play with . . .' and so on.	Model the process of how something can create positive or negative feelings – by commenting on how children handled things well – 'It was really helpful to open the door for Majid's mummy when she was carrying the boxes'.
Recognising that other children may feel differently about some things.	Children need visual reminders and auditory commentaries on acceptable and unacceptable behaviours – teaching them to show 'thumbs up' when they like something or 'thumbs down' or a face that is not smiling when they don't like something can help them to express feelings.	Offer a supportive commentary to the child who finds it hard to wait for a turn using the iPad, explaining that they will get a turn when the other person has finished the activity.
Recognising that rules for behaviour are about keeping me safe. Understanding how to stop and think before acting. Knowing who to turn to and what to do when my feelings are difficult to manage.	Involving children in thinking about ways to keep safe helps them to formulate and stick to rules that help everybody. Setting aside a chill out spot for children to go to by choice if they want to cool down gives children who are highly reactive time to stop and think before acting.	Discuss strategies for keeping calm and for calming down – accept ideas such as 'we could go for a walk, or run; we could sit quietly; we could breathe deeply; we could tell an adult'.

Practice review: Personal, Social and Emotional Development

Everyday practice

Consider the pedagogical responses below:

Five-year-old Alec has really enjoyed playing with two other children and an adult in a game based on the dinosaur Olympics games. He is very confident about choosing the correct number of counters to move his dinosaur forward by one, two, three or more spaces and he knows which of the different coloured dinosaurs is in the lead, and which are behind. He is triumphant when eventually he wins the game declaring as his dinosaur receives a gold medal on the podium: 'It's not winning that is important, it's taking part'. He is also able to identify that the yellow dinosaur has come second, winning the silver medal and that the bronze medal has been awarded to the green dinosaur because it came third in the race. However as they begin playing for a second time and it becomes obvious his dinosaur is going to be last, Alec becomes agitated, finally bursting into tears when his friend's red dinosaur receives the gold medal, and another dinosaur the silver medal, leaving his dinosaur to take the bronze medal because it finished last. After a while, still very upset, he says: 'It is about winning – I want to win!' When he is shouting Gemma puts her fingers in her ears and her face becomes tense.

a) The practitioner says to Alec, don't be upset – it's only a game – Gemma is your friend, you want her to win, don't you? And, I haven't won once yet, but you've got two medals now! Alec is inconsolable and says he wants his mummy and wishes he was at home.

b) The practitioner knows Alec well and recognises that this is a real challenge for him because he tries so hard to succeed in everything he does. S/he asks Alec to tell her how he is feeling but he is unable to articulate his feelings so s/he comments on his experience saying: 'I think you are really disappointed that you didn't win, aren't you? Especially when you were the gold medal winner last time – but Gemma and I didn't come first in the race that time or win the gold medal when you did'. S/he smiled remembering when Alec had said: 'It's not winning that is important, it's taking part' and reminds him that actually it had been fun playing the game and that it was probably just the last part that disappointed him. But Alec repeats that he wanted to win the game so the practitioner comforts him by saying that he had still been a winner – but that he had come third in the race; s/he also tells him that s/he understands that it isn't easy for him to deal with his anger and disappointment. S/he is aware that although Alec knows the right words to say (about winning and losing) he is really only practising them, like an actor, but s/he praises him for remembering to say them, recognising that knowing the words doesn't stop the feelings of disappointment. As he calms down s/he suggests to Alec that he might like to have a cool drink and a snack and then wash his hands and chill out with his favourite book.

Questioning everyday practice

Alec's learning characteristics:

Alec is passionately keen on succeeding and on winning the game – this shows that he is an active learner who loves to play and who experiences the race between the dinosaurs as something real. He is also very interested in details and not easily distracted showing he is involved and concentrating, other examples of Active learning, though he is finding it difficult to bounce back after experiencing difficulties.

Provocation for learning:

Whether the child or adult has initiated the play it is important for adults to remain focused on the opportunities for learning offered by the context.

Pedagogical response review

At (a), the reactive response, the practitioner has tried to appeal to Alec at a logical level – assuming that the five year old is capable of altruism – wanting his friend Gemma to succeed; s/he has also reminded him that he had won previously. S/he has not though, acknowledged his feelings nor shown empathy with his sense of disappointment at 'losing' the game. In (b), the considered response, the practitioner has acknowledged Alec's feelings and, importantly, has shown genuine concern about Alec's feelings, giving him words to describe them such as 'disappointed' and 'angry'. S/he then praises Alec for being able to talk about taking part being more important than winning and understands also that whilst Alec can do this there is a mismatch between his strong 'feelings' and his ability in 'cognitive/linguistic' domains. Empathising with him in this respect s/he knows he needs time to cool down.

The expression of feelings is important and whilst many children are capable of suppressing feelings this is an area that should be approached with considerable caution since the emphasis should be on children learning to deal with their feelings rather than simply ignoring them.

Effective practice

The aspects of PSED create a virtuous circle – making relationships supports children's self-confidence and self-awareness; whilst managing feelings and behaviour promotes children's ability to get along with others which in turn leads to improved relationships. For many children whose early emotional and social experiences are positive the skills involved in developing these three aspects appear to occur with little effort, however this is not necessarily the case since most responses are learned, including different ways of acting and interacting with others. Therefore these should be planned as part of the on-going teachable moments that occur regularly and frequently in the course of any session, in addition to there being explicit planning for learning in for example, Key Person groups, story sessions or 'thinking' sessions. Planning for this might include focuses on:

- **Why You Are Special** – this is most closely connected in the EYFS to the principle a Unique Child and helps every child understand their own individuality and involves understanding that to be different from others is to be celebrated – stories such as *On the Night You Were Born* (Tillman, 2005), create this sense of wonder at the uniqueness of every child.
- **Friends** – what they are like; why they are special; how we show friendship; why we include other children in our play; friendship in stories – this might include favourite toys or items children use as comforters – for example *Dogger* (Hughes, 2002), is a good example. Discussions might focus on opposites – feeling left out – compared with feeling you are part of the group. Friendship walls could show displays which identify attributes of friendliness – being kind,

sharing, taking turns, looking after somebody if they are upset, sad or worried and so on.

- **Family** – who is in our family; what we enjoy doing with different family members such as: baby brother, big sister, granddad and so on; our favourite meals, customs and things we like to do together; resolving differences. This might include making books or ebooks of 'my family', or inviting in different family members to tell a story, to demonstrate a skill, to bring along a pet, or to recount a real event.
- **Feelings** – different events, particularly changes, are often the source of untold anxieties for children and events such as a house move, a change in routine or the birth of a sibling can play havoc with children's emotions – books such as *I'm a Big Brother* or *I'm a Big Sister* (Cole, 1997) help children to consider the positive and negatives of the latter situation and provide suggestions of how adults can support children through such events.

Adult involvement

In order to ensure that children do develop pro-social skills they need to establish confidence in who they are and what they can do and know strategies for keeping themselves safe. Teaching skills in this area should not be left to chance – it is important to acknowledge how children feel in order to help them to process their feelings into acceptable actions. Understanding the effects of their own actions and behaviour on others may be new to some children who may have had few others to challenge their 'rights' whilst other children may be very familiar with such an approach. When children feel confident that adults will help them to deal with their feelings they learn the skills of stopping and thinking before acting. The nature of adult interaction is therefore highly significant since children 'learn what they live' and will base their understanding on the ways in which they see adults behaving – taking the time to gently talk through responses with a child will be far more productive than simply reacting to a child's behaviour. Reflecting on learning is a useful form of assessment and can be successfully integrated into discussions at the conclusion of a session – when children can comment on the things they enjoyed or that made them happy or the things they would change. The next chapters focus on children's learning in the specific areas of Literacy, Mathematics, Understanding the World and Expressive Arts and Design.

8 Literacy

Literacy is made up of two aspects: Reading and Writing. The roots of reading and writing begin with the development of communication skills: listening, attending, understanding and speaking; areas discussed in Chapters 6 and 7. It is significant that, according to a finding by an all-party review about barriers to reading: *'Parental involvement in their child's reading has been found to be the most important determinant of language and emergent literacy'* (Barker *et al.*, 2011: 9). And a further sobering finding from the same review revealed that *'The biggest difference between those who can read and those who find it a challenge is that those who can have been shown how much fun it can be by parents and other significant adults'* (ibid.: 6).

Reading

In the early years reading development emerges as children find out about and develop an interest in books and stories. Experiences such as repeating rhymes and joining in with jingles and playing with and finding out about words as well as sharing books, listening to and telling stories and narratives all create positive attitudes to reading. Together these pave the way for more specific instruction in reading skills, a necessary development from enjoyment, since it is known that *'Reading and writing abilities don't just happen. They are acquired, nurtured and refined through the acts of those who provide appropriate instructional contexts and support'* (CPIN, 2006).

Before any overt instruction in reading begins and without necessarily recognising it as such, those working with young children frequently engage in interactions which support children's early reading skills. For example, the following useful advice offered to parents by the US National Institute for Literacy sets out what parents might do to support this area; however this has been presented under two headings (Table 8.1), the second left blank for those working with babies and young children to use in analysing how each

Table 8.1 What parents and others can do to support reading development

Context for Learning	Interactions that Scaffold the Child's Learning
• *'Make reading a pleasure'* by reading to a child in a comfortable place; positioning the child so that they can see the pictures and the printed word; • *'Show enthusiasm'* by reading in a lively way and making expressions with hands and sounds with props; • *'Read to your* [their] *child often'* – reminding parents that the more they can read to their child the better – as long as the child is willing to listen; • *'Talk with your* [their] *child as you* [they] *read together'* commenting on what's happening in the story; • *'Encourage your* [their] *child to explore books'* allowing them to touch and hold books and turn the pages of books, or to lift flaps or look through holes in story books; finally suggesting that parents should • *'Read favourite books again and again'* (Armbuster *et al.*, 2006: 10) for children.	

occurs or is planned for in their setting, focusing on the interactions which support children's learning in this area.

The benefits of listening to stories and reading aloud (to infants and toddlers, though this holds true throughout the early years) are itemised in a High Scope briefing which indicates:

- *'Very young children first begin to read by interpreting the pictures*
- *Read-alouds enable children to have fun with words and learn more about language*
- *Reading to children helps focus on oral language*

- *Reading aloud to children eventually leads to children's understanding of written language (connecting spoken and written words)'* (Lockhart, 2012: 3)

Establishing children's interest and delight in stories, books, rhymes and poetry is a worthwhile investment for many reasons – not only for the pleasure this can bring in their young lives but also for the lifelong benefits that derive from learning to read. Reading therefore is not simply a skill but a key to a world of literacy and information in which all children have the right to participate.

Being read to provides the child with a model of what fluent readers do – and subtly helps them to distinguish between words and pictures and to understand conventions about directionality: from left to right and from top to bottom in English. Through this approach children also begin to understand the association between the written and spoken word and that their own and others' spoken words can be represented symbolically. Research has established that *'Conventional reading and writing skills that are developed in the years from birth to five have a clear and consistently strong relationship with later conventional literacy skills'* (Lonigan and Shanahan, 2008: vii) signalling the importance of this area for children's later learning. The most important predictive skills based on findings from a synthesis of the scientific research on the development of early literacy skills in children ages zero to five in the US were found to be:

- *'Alphabet knowledge: knowledge of the names and sounds associated with printed letters*
- *Phonological awareness: the ability to detect, manipulate, or analyse the auditory aspects of spoken language, (including the ability to distinguish or segment words, syllables or phonemes), independent of meaning*
- *Rapid automatic naming of letters or digits: the ability to randomly name a sequence of random letters or digits and random automatic naming of a sequence of repeating random sets of pictures of objects (e.g. car, tree, house, man) or colours*
- *Writing or writing name: the ability to write letters in isolation on request or to write one's own name*
- *Phonological memory: the ability to remember spoken information for a short period of time'* (ibid.: vii).

Whilst these are clearly important skills, it is notable that writers from the Canadian Language and Literacy Research Network indicate that whilst large-scale studies point to the importance of these early precursors to literacy these skills should not *'overshadow the importance of language development in the early years'* (Riley-Ayres and Barnett, 2012: 2) a worthwhile cautionary note.

However, whilst much can be gleaned by an alert, interested child, a review of effective programmes, in a meta-analysis relating to disadvantaged children and the academic gap in the UK, found that *early childhood programmes (for four-year-olds), with explicit literacy instruction and clear teaching objectives, improve children's school readiness* (Sharples *et al.*, 2011: 15), explaining the importance of a systematic approach to the teaching of reading. To explore such an approach is not possible within this publication; however the following brief overview may be helpful in focusing on approaches to the teaching of reading.

Reading development is based on skills and attitudes which range from simple to complex. Beginning with establishing a love of books children should be supported to cultivate listening skills allowing them to develop phonological awareness – described in terms of a continuum beginning with:

- *oral songs,*
- *sentence segmentation,*
- *syllable segmentation and blending* as well as
- *blending and segmenting individual phonemes* (Chard and Dickson, undated).

Approaches to teaching reading usually run in parallel with many precursory reading skills as part of a literacy curriculum where stories are shared and recalled and in which children are introduced to print conventions such as the front cover, the name of the author, title of the book and so on. Closely linked to communication and language development any structured approach for younger children may focus on sound discrimination in programmes such as Phase One Letters and Sounds (DCSF, 2008a) – which includes environmental, instrumental and body percussion; rhythm and rhyme, alliteration, voice sounds and oral blending and segmenting (ibid.). Identifying strategies to support the teaching of early reading however, members of the International Reading Association suggest that whilst phonemic awareness (being able to hear, identify and deploy sounds or phonemes in speech) is auditory it also has links with phonics and may involve the use of print.

Early reading experiences

Experiences (in addition to those discussed previously) that support children's interest in becoming a reader are set out in Table 8.2 – consider how planning for these reflects different strategies for supporting children's learning.

Table 8.2 Experiences that support children's reading

Contexts for Learning about Reading	Interactions that Scaffold the Child's Learning
• Listening to stories	
• Sharing books (fiction and non-fiction)	
• Identifying favourite characters and/or events in stories and talking about them	
• Talking about pictures in story books	
• Talking about photographs	
• Talking about pictures in non-fiction books	
• Developing an awareness that print carries meaning	
• Noticing and talking about environmental print – shops names and logos are familiar to children; so are names of TV programmes and/or characters	
• Recalling and retelling stories in order	
• Focusing on the direction of text when it is being read	
• Exploring rhyming strings	
• Blending sounds together	
• Identifying print such as the title of a book, name of illustrator and the blurb	
• Developing phonic knowledge to orally **blend** simple consonant-vowel-consonant (CVC) words, for example: sat, pin, tap.	
• Developing phonic knowledge to orally **segment** simple consonant-vowel-consonant (CVC) words, for example: sat, pin, tap.	
• Taking part in shared reading sessions.	

Providing pictures, props and other peripherals that support the child in connecting with characters and events from stories is also powerful. These might be connected with favourite characters; music associated with particular stories or characters or photographs of children sharing books or engaging in role play connected with them – such as *We're Going on a Bear Hunt* (Rosen, 1989) or other stories that young children enjoy because of the associated sounds and actions as well as the introduction of tension and problem resolution.

The Independent Review of Reading, undertaken by Sir Jim Rose (Rose, 2006) to identify the most direct route to young children becoming skilled readers drew on evidence from both the US and Australia to conclude that the best practice for beginner readers provides them with a rich curriculum 'fostering speaking, listening, reading and writing' and that '*despite uncertainties in research findings*' the case for systematic phonic work was 'overwhelming', citing that synthetic phonics offered the vast majority of young children '*the most direct route to becoming skilled readers and writers*'. He identified that beginning readers should be taught four things, visually:

- Grapheme-phoneme correspondences (that is letter/sound correspondence – the alphabetic principle) in a clearly defined, incremental sequence.
- To synthesise or blend phonemes/sounds in order all through a word to read it (Ofsted, 2011).
- To segment words into their constituent phonemes in order to spell them
- That blending and segmenting are reversible processes (Rose, 2006).

Whatever approach is taken to reading it is important to ensure that teaching episodes are short and enjoyable and multi-sensory; that activities are appropriate and differentiated so that children experience success and that children have opportunities to apply their learning in meaningful, independent activities. As well as teaching early reading skills, many settings provide excellent opportunities to encourage reading. These range from the provision of beautiful, well-kept books in an environment that invites the child to engage with them, to events that may shape a child's view of reading for the rest of their lives such as meeting and working with a children's book author; celebrating World Book Day by dressing up in character along with all the practitioners, and watching and taking part in story dramatisations.

For slightly older children in reception classes consider the predominant approach to reading set out below (Table 8.3) and then the interactions that scaffold children's learning. These will be based on promoting a variety of skills involving several interconnected approaches.

Table **8.3** Experiences that support children as readers in reception

Context for Learning	Interactions that Scaffold the Child's Learning
• Reading and Sharing Stories one-to-one and in small groups;	
• Independent Reading – involving children's own interpretations and recall of stories that have been enjoyed;	
• Modelled Reading – with a text that is visible to groups of children and in which the teacher describes their own strategies for decoding words and thinking about meaning;	
• A programme of phonics instruction to support reading development. In reception classes the recommendation has been to continue with phonics of the type presented in Phase One of Letters and Sounds at the same time as introducing the 44 phonemes of the English language in a systematic sequence which quickly leads children to independent reading using phonic strategies;	
• Learning 'sight words' which do not conform to predictable phonic pronunciation, often referred to as 'tricky' words;	
• Shared Reading where children and teacher read together focusing on different aspects of texts such as *comprehension, concepts of print, decoding strategies and language of books*' (CCEA, 2006: 9);	
• Guided, or Emergent Reading which allows children, in small groups, to focus on reading for meaning.	

How such sessions are organised will depend on individual circumstances including whether children are older or younger and on individual choice of approaches to reading. The detail provided for Reading in *Development Matters* for children from 30–50 months and for those of 40–60 months is helpful in considering methods for developing reading with older children. The learning requirement for this area is also useful:

> *'Literacy development involves encouraging children to link sounds and letters and to begin to read and write. Children must be given access to a wide range of reading materials (books, poems, and other written materials) to ignite their interest'.*
>
> (DfE, 2012: 5)

Beyond this it is worthwhile considering the explanatory note, attached to the ELG for Reading, explaining the content of the Early Learning Goal which suggests that reading involves the following:

1 *'The child uses cues such as pictures, letter/word recognition, knowledge of the story or context and reading for meaning, in order to help them comprehend a range of . . . texts.*
2 *The child blends and segments words independently and applies their phonic knowledge to regular and irregular unfamiliar words.*
3 *The child shares his or her ideas about what they have read with others'*
   (STA, 2012: 27).

This suggests the focus should be upon ensuring a child understands what they are reading rather than that they simply develop the ability to decode words. An issue highlighted in the national EYFS data for Reading when children's outcomes for 'linking sounds and letters' (DfE/SFR 23, 2012) exceeded those for 'reading', showed that whilst 83% of children attained a good level of development in Linking Sounds and Letters (phonic knowledge), fewer children (79%), achieved a good level of development for Reading. Clearly if phonics teaching is successful children will understand how to apply their learning – so time for application of learning should be built in – since learning a particular grapheme-phoneme correspondence (GPC) within one context does not necessarily transfer to different contexts. It is important also to ensure that children enjoy their learning in this area since if children are to continue reading learning to read should be an enjoyable experience.

Finally, reading is about gaining access to literature of all kinds; there is no question that it is necessary to develop reading skills, however, the way this is achieved is highly significant since teaching children to read should leave them 'wanting' to read, something that may be lost if too much emphasis is placed on skills rather than on reading for pleasure and information.

Writing

Writing is intrinsically connected with reading and is inspired by the knowledge that the written word conveys meaning. Reaching this understanding is a lengthy process which is enhanced by seeing writing modelled by experts (practitioners, older children and parents). Prior to this however it is important to note that mark-making is a precursor to writing and that *'Evidence found that preschool variables significantly associated with writing competence at school entry included mother's education, family size, parental assessment of the child's writing ability and a measure of home writing activities. The latter was still significant at the age of seven'* (DfE, 2012a: 3), once again stressing the importance to children's learning of parents who are involved and interested.

Recent discussions of children's literacy affirm the importance and influence of environmental print on young children's early writing, whereas in the past this area was considered more important for early reading. It is now recognised, however, that *'environmental print can stimulate writing'* since *'children often imitate the writing they see, such as notices or notes left for others'* (Nutbrown and Hannon, 2011: 3). Supporting this view an analysis of research into the environmental print/writing relationship suggests that academically advantaged children recognise more environmental print logos than their at-risk peers and that notwithstanding this *'all children benefit from exposure to print in their environment'* (McMahon Giles and Wellhousen Tucks, 2010: 23). When discussing the stages of developmental writing through which children may progress, the Californian Instructional Networks Pre-school (CPIN, 2006) guidance outlines five stages:

Table 8.4 Stages of writing based on CPIN presentation: Developmental Writing (CPIN website)

1. **Awareness, Exploration or Role Play Writing**	Comprising drawing and scribbling: this would approximate to early mark-making where the differences between words and pictures are not apparent.
	(CPIN suggests that at this stage children are coming to terms with a new aspect of language, that is that words can be represented symbolically and they *'experiment with marks on*

(Continued)

Table 8.4 Continued

		paper with the intention of communicating a message or emulating adult writing' (CPIN, 2006). However, a distinction between writing and drawing is that in these early stages drawing is made to stand for writing; children believe that their drawings convey a message and children will 'read' their drawings as if there were writing on them. The explanation for this seems to be that the child is coming to an understanding of the concept of symbolic understanding. Indicators of this stage are described as: '*The Writer* • *assigns a message to own symbols* • *understands that writing and drawing are different* • *is aware print carries meaning, and* • *shows beginning awareness of directionality*' (ibid.).
2.	**Emergent or Experimental Writing**	Comprising Early Emergent and Emergent/Experimental this stage includes the representation of 'letter-like forms' which although not actually letters/graphemes look similar. During this stage real letters do emerge and are represented in long, unbroken strings. Likening this stage to building with blocks it is suggested that the child is as yet unaware of there being only 26 letters of the alphabet.
3.	**Transitional or Early Writing**	Characterised by representations focusing on topics of children's own interests. The use of single letters to write words (phonemic spelling), for example: W R (to express 'we are') shows increasing awareness of language sounds. In this stage there is heavy reliance on the most obvious sounds of a word and the purposes of some writing is understood by the child – such as we write a list to remember items, or a sign to give an instruction or information.

4. **Conventional**	The three phases above lead, over time, towards the complimentary skills of conventional and proficient writing, reflecting the child's familiarity with much of the writing process including an awareness of different forms and purposes for writing, and familiarity with structure and use of punctuation.
5. **Proficient Writing**	

Children's writing development, is generally understood as a continuum from mark-making through to conventional writing (early mark-making also involves drawing) and is important when considering a child's present understanding and in planning for the next steps in their learning. Writing development has also been conceptualised in terms of a 'simple view' and a 'not so simple view' (Berninger and Amtmann, 2003: 323–334), the latter taking account of information from brain imaging studies. Involving three key features, the 'not so simple view of writing' model involves: **text generation**, to write words or sentences, where having identified what they wish to say the child '*"hears" the word – either aloud or in their head – and mentally divides it into its individual composite phonemes*', they then, '*match the letters or graphemes to corresponding phonemes*' (DfE website SPLD resources, 2012), applying their phonic knowledge to compose writing through **transcription**, (involving handwriting, keyboarding and spelling); and utilising, at the same time, **executive functions**, needed to:

- '*Plan sentences and remember them long enough to write them.*
- *Say a word out loud and remember it long enough to spell it.*
- *Remember the correct motor process to produce a letter or word, at the same time as you learn a spelling.*
- *Plan a storyline and compose the story.*
- *Organise and present key points in a text logically.*
- *Keep track of your progress in a piece of writing.*
- *Correctly copy a word from a dictionary or word bank.*' (ibid.)
- Gradually automate low level processes (handwriting and spelling) so that resource can be made available for more demanding processes such as composition and planning.
- Gradually improve the automaticity for spelling and handwriting, which is particularly useful for pupils who struggle with transcriptional aspects of writing.

The process of writing is intricate not least because it involves both the physical aspects involved in holding and using writing tools, as well as the cognitive aspects of knowing that symbols (graphemes) represent sounds which singly or in combination can create words, which must be represented through symbols. Comparing the 'expected' level for children's writing (in the EYFSP exemplification of the Writing ELG) with the stages set out above, indicates that the expected level is between the Transitional/Early Writing and Conventional writing stages (CPIN, 2006). Similar developmental trajectories for writing exist and can be useful for comparison for example: First Steps Writing Continuum (Education Department of Western Australia, 1997), and many integrated schemes exist including Read, Write Inc. (Oxford University Press website).

The ELG for writing is, that children *use phonic knowledge to write words in ways which match spoken sounds*. Children write some *irregular common words* and *simple sentences which can be read by themselves and others. Some words are spelt correctly and others are phonetically plausible* (DfE, 2012: 9). Reference to the word 'sentence' in the ELG may be confusing and should be considered carefully in light of the examples provided (STA, 2013a). The EYFSP exemplification identifies the following examples as indicative of the 'expected' level for a child to achieve in the Writing ELG:

Oscar's Sign

'*Oscar had spent over 40 minutes building a giant's castle with a small group. It was nearing the end of the session and he was keen that it was not taken down. "We need a notice now" he announced. "I'm going to make it!" He organised himself in the writing area. This is what he wrote! His notice read*' (STA, 2013a) '**Pleze doant Brak the casle**'.

This shows that Oscar understood the purpose for writing; he was able to compose what he wanted to say and to use his phonic knowledge to segment the sounds to write:

Pleze: Please
doant: don't
Brak: break
casle: castle

His knowledge of tricky words allowed him to recall the word 'the' and to write it correctly.

It is notable that whilst Oscar's writing contains both a capital letter and a full stop these features are not necessary in achievement of the ELG at the 'expected' level.

'M's' Story

This example of writing at the 'expected' level in the EYFS is accompanied by the following explanation: '*The rich resources in the writing area inspired "M" to write her own version of the traditional tale (from a previous story telling session)*' (ibid.) what M wrote was: '**Onec a pon o time ther livd a boy with his mumy he tuc his cow to the marcit he sor a od man who galv the magic beens mumy fraad the beens a wai**'. The practitioner interpreted the child's words as follows:

'Once upon a time there lived a boy with his mummy he took his cow to the market he saw an old man who gave him the magic beans mummy threw the magic beans away'.

Analysis of 'M's' writing shows s/he is able to write common irregular words including: 'the', 'to', 'magic'; 'once'; that some words are also spelt correctly: 'time', 'he', 'a', 'man', 'boy'; 'his' and that others are phonetically plausible, visually: – 'a pon'; 'ther'; 'livd'; 'mumy'; 'tuc'; 'marcit'; 'sor'; 'od'; 'beens'; 'fraad'; 'a wai'.

It is notable that whilst M's writing contains a story there is neither a capital letter nor a full stop, these features are not necessary in achievement of the ELG at the 'expected' level, and that whilst his/her writing expresses several ideas there are no obvious sentences.

The emphasis in both examples above and the remaining exemplification is on developing children's confidence as writers. The more technical aspects of correct letter formation and of punctuation are not emphasised at this stage, which is extremely positive since although these are ultimately significant, in the early stages of writing children need to 'find their voice' – in other words transcription aspects of writing can be taught and children will at some point incorporate these into their writing but before this – they need to write without being concerned too greatly with these aspects of written communication.

Experiences to support writing

In addition to all the experiences discussed elsewhere including those relating to the Prime Areas, particularly Physical Play to promote gross and fine motor skills, the following experiences support children to develop writing skills when adult interaction is focused appropriately – you may wish to consider the following alongside Table 5.2:

Table 8.5 Experiences which support the development of writing skills

Context for Learning	Interactions that Scaffold the Child's Learning
• Drawing and mark-making	
• Free access in all areas both in and out of doors to a range of mark-making materials	
• Looking at and talking about the marks they and others make	
• Seeing, talking about and 'spotting' writing in the environment, such as signs on pavements near school: 'Stop, look, listen'.	
• Access to labels, alphabets, tricky word displays, dictionaries and writing materials in a well-resourced mark-making area	
• Access to a range of items that a writer might want to use in book making – such as split pins, elastic bands, hole punches, stamp pads and stampers, different weights and colours of paper, scissors and so on	
• Observing writers writing for real purposes such as – a parent completing a form; a practitioner writing a list of ingredients for making play dough; a doctor signing a prescription and so on.	
• Hearing proficient writers talking about their own writing – for example: 'I am leaving a finger space between the word "little" and "pigs" so that I can see the two words properly.'	
• Taking part in shared writing sessions where a proficient writer scribes and models the different aspects of conventional writing.	
• Receiving praise and encouragement for independent writing attempts	

• Reading aloud own marks or writing to an interested adult or older child or a peer	
• Being supported to write through guided writing sessions where the adult enables the child to think about what they know about writing and apply their knowledge to write something of significance – such as Oliver's sign described above.	

Emergent writers are inspired by surfaces large and small and by materials that respond to touch – these might include chalk boards, interactive whiteboards, glitter, gloop or sand in trays – the addition of styluses and combs can make mark-making in these materials great fun as will the provision of different sized sticks for use in mud; large paint brushes and rollers offer coverage too on surfaces outdoors, as well as the more conventional twig pens, felt tips, ball pens, pencils, charcoal, pastels and crayons. Additionally many interactive 'apps' also offer very simple and rewarding free-style mark-making in programmes such as Doodoo Lite, KaleidoBalls, Pastels and many more; tried and tested magnetic boards and letters can also be used as a means of writing by older children. The focus of the following chapter is Mathematics.

9   Mathematics

Compared with Literacy, there has often been reluctance in the early years to develop children's mathematical skills to the same extent as reading and writing skills. This may reflect the preferences and interests of early years practitioners or the fact that some are not confident mathematicians. Furthermore little recent guidance has been offered to support mathematical pedagogy in the early years, although the Independent Review of Mathematics provided extremely sound recommendations, suggesting that: '*Central to effective mathematical pedagogy in the early years is fostering children's natural interest in numeracy, problem solving, reasoning, shapes and measures. Children should be given opportunities in a broad range of contexts, both indoors and outdoors, to explore, enjoy, learn, practise and talk about their developing mathematical understanding. Such experiences develop a child's confidence in tackling problem solving, asking probing questions, and pondering and reasoning answers across their learning. Vitally important is ensuring that children's mathematical experiences are fun, meaningful and build confidence*' (Williams, 2008: 34). In order to support children's development in this area, pedagogy should therefore be focused not only on skills and knowledge but also on developing positive attitudes towards mathematical learning and ensuring that children have support to develop their problem-solving skills.

Following the introduction of the EYFS (2007) a small scale research project focusing on teaching, learning and play in reception classes with twenty children and eight teachers (TACTYC, 2011) identified that compared with whole class literacy sessions which accounted for 8.0% of children's time their time in whole class mathematics sessions was significantly less (0.8%). In addition it was noted that the amount of time boys and girls spent in small group sessions was considerably less for girls than boys in literacy and maths sessions – the boys spending 4.1% of time doing maths compared with girls spending 2.8% of their time and in literacy girls spent 0.5% of their time compared with boys who spent 4.4% of their time in this type of activity. Notwithstanding the size of sample nor the intended focus of the research it is interesting that these findings reveal that less time was devoted to mathematics and more time to literacy overall in the reception classes (the role of the National Literacy Strategy is considered key in this); as well as the fact that boys were involved for more time in more small group sessions for both areas of learning: literacy and mathematics – clearly this may relate to any number of reasons including teachers' concerns about boys' outcomes in the EYFS which, since records began, have been consistently lower than those of girls across all areas of learning (DfE/SFR 23, 2012). However it is important to note that whilst teaching a large group of children may have some benefits – there is good evidence to suggest '*that small-group instruction has been found to be an effective context for enhancing young children's learning*' (Cross *et al.*, 2009: 247). This suggests if less time were spent in whole group teaching and more on working with smaller groups capitalising on teachable moments would be more possible since adults would have greater opportunities to scaffold children's learning more effectively.

The foundations of learning in mathematics are closely related to language and vocabulary acquisition as well as to concept development. Set out as the learning requirements for this area the following few words, whilst deceptively simple, are the basis of children's mathematical learning in the EYFS and beyond, providing: '*children with opportunities to develop and improve their skills in counting, understanding and using numbers, calculating simple addition and subtraction problems; and to describe shapes, spaces, and measures*' (DfE, 2012: 5). The basis of these skills begin early, and, although counter-intuitive to what many adults believe, it is clear that babies and young children recognise differences in quantity, make predictions based on observation, and hypothesise about probability. One study, intended to establish babies' ability to select 'more', showed that when 10 and 12 month olds observed an experimenter placing crackers into two opaque containers thirteen out of sixteen children from each age group preferred the container holding two rather than one cracker, indicating their ability to differentiate between the amounts (Feigenson *et al.*, 2002).

A major analysis of young children's mathematical learning in the US showed this to be the case, indicating though, that '*infants' early knowledge of number is largely implicit*' and pointing out that since research with babies and infants does not normally use number words '*learning the number words and relating them to sets of objects is a major new kind of learning done by toddlers and pre-schoolers at home*' (Cross *et al.*, 2009: 66) [and subsequently when they attend settings]. However, for a number of reasons, this type of mathematical understanding is often not recognised and because of concerns about whether teaching mathematics is appropriate for young children teaching can either become very limited or too narrowly focused on, for example, the development of counting aloud. Whereas, a broader approach can be adopted when opportunities for mathematical learning are seen as valid – these occur most frequently in the context of children's everyday experiences. Therefore it is important to ensure that young children's early learning of numbers begins with their own experiences. Mathematics is made up of two aspects in the EYFS: Numbers and Shape, Space and Measures, which are explored in the following sections.

Numbers

The events most connected with learning numbers for the youngest children are those which have meaning for them – initially linked to themselves and the environment and deriving from playful interactions with practitioners and other children. For example, talking about numbers as part of everyday interaction might begin with looking in a mirror and pointing to a baby's nose noting there is: 'one' and counting each of their eyes or ears to arrive at 'two'; or singing a counting song whilst going up or downstairs.

Building the concept of a quantity, such as 'two' might then occur when discussions focus on whether the child has one piece of cucumber for each hand or one shoe for each foot, or in discussions of their age. Beginning with these everyday interactions young children develop familiarity with the idea that numbers describe or symbolise the abstraction of quantity, though they may not understand the amount represented by a particular number. This initial understanding must be extended so that eventually this becomes integrated into a more comprehensive understanding of the relationship between the words and the quantities involved. An analysis of Numbers in *Development Matters* (DfE/EE, 2012) shows that early mathematical development is linked to understanding very small numbers such as 'three' and detecting differences when these change. This process leads to accurately identifying a small number of items such as two or three, integrating the idea of the understanding that *'the last number I say in the count is the name used to represent the size of the group'* (DCSF, 2009a: 20). In order to do this the child must remember which items have been touched and which items remain uncounted – children frequently miss out some items or count some items more than once since understanding the counting principle takes considerable practice. At the same time they are learning that the number of items in a set remains the same wherever they start counting from – for example counting can begin at any point in a circle of pebbles provided the starting point is remembered; the key to accuracy is to count each pebble only once. The importance of counting for a real purpose should always be emphasised as well as the usefulness of one-to-one correspondence in daily activities. This might include finding out how many children are in the key group – by counting pictures of the children, or counting the number of fish for each player to find out which child has won a fishing game, or modelling how to count out the number of bean bags thrown into a bucket by each child and so on.

Counting items in a line is known to be easier for children initially than when items are bundled together or cannot be touched or moved, such as buildings or songs. Understanding that counting forwards is a way of adding one, whilst counting backwards allows them to 'take one away' from a quantity such as five supports the child's understanding of addition and subtraction. Hence activities such as singing rhymes, for example, Five Little Ducks, can be helpful in establishing children's early understanding of addition and subtraction operations. Also useful is a string of balls which can be moved so that different groups can be separated which supports the understanding of partitioning when children begin to learn that numbers can be broken into sets. A pair of socks can be used to show a set of two which can be separated into smaller sets: one and one. A row of ten balls can be made into sets of five and five, or five lots of two.

Recognition that the number names always follow in order becomes apparent through discussions and through access to and use of numerals pegged to a fence or wall where they can be moved and ordered correctly or through number lines. An example of a child's understanding of the number order is provided in the EYFSP exemplification indicating a child having reached this understanding at an 'expected' level, that is, at the end of the EYFS:

> During a hunt for the dinosaur egg Harry knew which number clues he needed to find next. 'You start at number 1, then you need to look for number 2, then number 3, then number 4 until you find all ten clues'.
>
> (STA, 2013b: 2)

The concepts of 'more than', 'less than' and 'the same as' develop initially from baby and toddlerhood when 'more' is a very useful word used as a shortcut to explain that the child has not had enough of things such as different foods, or of being read to, or being pushed on a swing. This understanding is extended through discussions about events such as the outcome of a game where the winner might have collected more tiles, or counters, or cards.

Another skill which follows, when children have developed fluent counting skills is '*"perceptual subitising" which refers to the child's ability to instantly recognise and name the number of objects in a set*' (Cross *et al.*, 2009), this is often demonstrated when a child 'knows' a number of objects within a set, for example when a child sees three stones they may not need to count since the quantity is instantly recognisable to the child.

Counting and matching games with real items to manipulate are known to enhance mathematical learning – since these offer the possibility of moving and placing items in different sequences. Sequencing underpins the child's ability to understand pattern – placing beads of different colours in a row becomes a pattern as the child notices that a series is emerging such as red, blue, red, blue. In this process children are learning to match different items and to compare items so that they can classify items into particular groups or sets because of properties such as size, shape or function.

A comprehensive review of the literature in relation to young children's mathematical development points to the apparent simplicity of foundational mathematics which begins in early childhood, highlighting the important role of effective pedagogy in this area. This review showed that young children need to develop an understanding of the four dimensions of number as shown below, though the last of these (4) whilst important in the longer term is more significant towards the end of the EYFS:

> These involve
> 1   **Cardinality**: Children's knowledge of cardinality (how many are in a set) increases as they learn specific number words for sets of objects they see (I want two crackers).
> 2   **Number word list**: Children begin to learn the ordered list of number words as a sort of chant separate from any use of that list in counting objects.
> 3   **1-to-1 counting correspondences**: When children do begin counting, they must use one-to-one counting correspondences so that each object is paired with exactly one number word.
> 4   **Written number symbols**: Children learn written number symbols.
> (ibid. 129)
> **NB:** (In the EYFS item 4 in the above list refers to recognition of numbers, not to the writing of numbers, though this may also happen.)

Essentially the dominant focus in learning about numbers in the EYFS is on helping children develop confidence in and understanding of the connection between the first of the three elements above; whilst developing strategies for representing numbers through mark-making are seen as skills which precede writing numerals and learning to write numbers. Interestingly whilst in *Development Matters* it is indicated that a child of 40–60 months: '*Records, using marks that they can interpret and explain*' (DfE/EE, 2012: 34) this is not a requirement in achievement of the ELG for Numbers, since the latter states: '*children count reliably with numbers from 1 to 20, place them in order and say which number is one more or one less than a given number. Using quantities and objects, they add and subtract two single-digit numbers and count on or back to find the answer. They solve problems, including doubling, halving and sharing*' (DfE, 2012: 9).

It is important not to underestimate what this involves and essential to bear in mind that fluency in number takes a considerable time to become embedded – and that whilst children encounter numbers in their lives from a very young age learning about numbers is not linear since, as mathematics guidance for the original EYFS (DfES, 2007) proposed: *'Children's learning of numbers is holistic, and they do not learn numbers in the traditional order . . . Larger numbers fascinate some children (often boys); . . . who often talk about '100' or '1000' and know that it is a 'big' number'* (DCSF, 2009a: 19). Beginning to develop this understanding of numbers up to and beyond ten involves the base ten: *'The system is called a base 10 system because it uses 10 distinct digits and is based on repeated groupings by 10. The use of only 10 digits to write any counting number, no matter how large, is achieved by using place value. That is, the meaning of a digit in a written number depends (in a very specific way) on its placement'* (Cross *et al.*, 2009: 28). In order to support children to understand and use this system it is important to ensure that teaching and learning takes place when children are curious about something and also that children begin to recognise and look for patterns as they occur, for example lining up toy cars by size, big, little, big, little, or noticing a number pattern on a number line.

Number lines (which can be placed next to one another in tens) can be interesting for high attaining children to explore, and the provision of pebbles, buttons or marbles in large amounts can also provoke children's interests as can commercial products such as Numicon or Cuisenaire which support exploration of the base ten. Arguing in favour of such explorations the US Committee on Early Childhood Mathematics noted that whilst practitioners spent a great deal of time in exploring the calendar this does not help in terms of children's understanding of the base ten, stating:

> Although the calendar may be useful in helping children begin to understand general concepts of time, such as 'yesterday' and 'today,' or plan for important events, such as field trips or visitors, these are not core mathematical concepts. The main problem with the calendar is that the groups of seven days in the rows of a calendar have no useful mathematical relationship to the number 10, the building block of the number system. Therefore, the calendar is not useful for helping students learn the base 10 patterns; other visual and conceptual approaches using groups of 10 are needed because these patterns of groups of 10 are foundational.
>
> (Cross *et al.*, 2009: 241)

Clearly this is an issue for more able children who do find large numbers fascinating; developing the basis for understanding these numbers begins as soon as the child discovers numbers beyond eleven when they are beginning to work out the next number proposing, for example, that 'five teen' follows fourteen, or asking what number follows 19. Therefore, capitalising on opportunities that arise, to sing and say number rhymes and to use number words, and to draw children's attention to quantity should be the focus for teaching and learning in this aspect of mathematics.

The following statements, from a National Strategies publication (cited also as areas for potential difficulties), present some key skills connected with number words and numerals, which link to the EYFS outcomes for this area:

- *'Knowing the number names in order*
- *Counting forwards and backwards in ones*
- *Recognising, saying and identifying numbers*
- *Ordering numbers*
- *Knowing the number that comes before or after'* (DCSF, 2009b: 4).

And, for counting sets the following skills and potential difficulties are amongst those identified in the same publication:

- *'Keeping track of the objects counted*
- *Recognising that the number associated with the last object touched is the total number of objects*
- *Counting things you cannot move, touch or see, or counting objects of different sizes*
- *Knowing when to stop when counting out a number of objects from a larger set*
- *Recognising small number of objects without counting (subitising)*
- *Recognising that, if a group of objects already counted, is rearranged, the total number stays the same*
- *Partitioning and recombining small groups of objects*
- *Counting on or back to add or subtract'* (ibid.: 10).

Experiences to support Numbers

In addition to all of the processes discussed previously:

Learning number names and developing one-to-one correspondence
- Saying and singing number rhymes, sometimes with the addition of props, to learn the number sequence for example: 'One potato, two potato, three potato, four'; or, 'One, two buckle my shoe, three four knock at the door'; or, 'This Old Man'.
- Counting in context of everyday activities – such as when climbing stairs; fastening buttons; playing games

- Finding numbers in the environment such as door numbers, car numbers, bus numbers, numbers on signs, numbers on price tags; numbers on a lift; door entry system; door; telephone numbers and so on.

Sorting, categorising or counting and identifying more/less/the same
Use everyday routines such as:

- tidy up time when children put all the little bears in the basket or similar blocks next to one another on the shelf;
- snack times when children know clean cups are put on the tray and used cups go in the bucket;
- lunch times when a child might count the number of Spiderman lunch boxes or Roary the Racing Car lunch boxes; or how many children are having hot or cold lunches;
- home time when a child might count how many children have made a model to take home.

Counting, ordering and comparing amounts
Games or activities (either child-initiated or adult-guided – the first is better because children will be more motivated to succeed in a game of their own choosing or one they have devised themselves), for example:

- counting a series of moves forward or backward in a board game; or
- giving the same number of cake cases to themselves and another child, and then, when mixture is added, finding they each need one more to accommodate the mixture.
- Deciding which team has thrown more balls into a target tyre by matching all the red and blue balls.

Oral counting on to add and counting back to subtract
- Saying and singing number rhymes, sometimes with the addition of props, to link addition with: 'Five little people in a flying saucer', 'Five little monkeys'; 'Ten little speckled frogs';
- Sharing books where lots of different pictures provide opportunities for discussion – for example 'You Choose' (Sharratt and Goodhart, 2000) is a book which provides endless opportunities for discussion about what kind of a 'house' a child might choose to live in or what picture they would like to have for their wall – children readily refer to number when this is modelled by an adult – who might say: 'I wouldn't like that one but I would like those two'.
- Activities and experiences such as role play, building with blocks, books that present numerical information whilst being intrinsically

interesting – for example Elmer (McKee, 1989) where the mathematical information is secondary to the story.

Manipulating and separating items into groups
- Access to a range of resources that can be moved, such as twigs, sticks and pebbles which can be arranged in groups, piles or bundles and counted out, separated into sets or series.

Tallying to keep count
- Recording the number of times a child has successfully kicked or thrown a ball into a net successfully; devising ways to show how many animals belong in each pen in a farm by drawing circles or faces, dots or lines, for example. This learning is linked in part to the second aspect of Mathematics: Shape, Space and Measures which follows.

Shape, Space and Measures

Shape, Space and Measures is an extensive area involving learning about:

- Shape
- Size
- Weight
- Capacity
- Position
- Distance
- Time
- Money
- Patterns, *and associated*
- Mathematical vocabulary.

Described in the explanatory note accompanying the associated ELG, outcomes at the end of the EYFS are: '*The child uses everyday language to share thinking about size, weight, capacity, position, distance, time and money. The child demonstrates that they understand that one quantity is different from another even if they do not know the comparative term. The child is able to recognise and describe patterns and notices them in the environment. Using a range of media and resources the child makes patterns. The child notices and describes everyday objects and shapes using appropriate mathematical language*' (STA, 2012: 28). This suggests that children need many real-life, practical experiences that engage their interest and prompt their mathematical thinking.

Shape can be viewed both holistically and as separate parts; early shape awareness tends to include 2D shapes in the child's immediate environment such as circles, squares and rectangles seen in pictures, food packaging and other items. Form boards containing common shapes including triangles also reveal that when an item is removed the same shape is left in relief – a space which can be covered or infilled. The parts of shapes that are most often known by young children refer to the number of sides, whilst older children can often quantify these as well as the number of corners (vertices) (Cross *et al.*, 2009). As well as noticing shapes, children often use 3D blocks and recycled materials such as boxes, kitchen roll tubes, bottle tops and other items in their play and in designing and making structures which leads to considerations of the position of different items in relation to one another – for example using a rectangular block to form the base of a house to which a triangular block is added to create a roof. Older children will also gain good understanding of capacity by tidying away blocks and other materials into a space which is designed to contain them: silhouettes make correct placement easier.

Almost every play experience has the potential for learning in this area however if mathematising does not form part of adults' interactions with children then opportunities can easily be missed for helping children to question areas of potential interest or to find ways to solve mathematical problems. Significantly, unless children are given the freedom to make 'mistakes' their learning can easily be stalled – so, for example, if a child is estimating how much material will be needed to cover a den they may have to try lots of different pieces of material before they find one which is suitable for the job; standing back and allowing this to happen, or indeed encouraging this, can seem difficult for adults whose experience in making this judgement is much greater; overcoming the desire to intervene before a child solves such a problem can be very tempting.

Providing children with the vocabulary to express their mathematical thinking in such an investigation should be embedded as part of the adult-child interaction and referred to subsequently in discussions with the child as part of documenting their processes. This approach encourages the child to think mathematically and to develop an understanding of the use and application of mathematics in their lives. The use of this approach was evident in a school I visited where a four-year-old boy in a reception class who had been building a complex structure alongside friends in the outdoor area, paused, picked up a clipboard and pencil and commenced drawing, however moments later he moved back, at which point an interested adult began to talk to him and the boy explained he had had to move further back to in order to see the whole building; he had recognised that being close up provided only a partial view of the structure. This led to discussions of perspective and the introduction of a text written by a local author on architecture.

A girl was also observed on a light coloured cover where she was carefully placing stones into an outline she had created of a dolphin (Figure 9.1) – she selected stone after stone in order to fill the shape, learning in the process about shape, size, position, and pattern, and in later discussions with adults documenting her learning was able to discuss how she had addressed particular problems such as finding the right stones to fit the dolphin's mouth.

Examples drawn from the exemplification of the 'expected' level in the EYFSP for this area include: play with objects where in developing an understanding of the concept of size children compare sizes of animals or the heights of towers, or how much material is needed to create a headband of the right size for a child, as well as examples of measurement with non-standard units (blocks) and with standard units – a centimetre rule. Understanding of weight is illustrated through use of items such as Unifix, conkers or pebbles to create equal amounts on balance beams or buckets; pulling another child behind him on a bike revealed a child's understanding of weight – when he told his friend 'you're too heavy'. Understanding of money largely takes place in role play whilst concepts such as time are developed through discussions of significant events, dates and times in children's lives, revealed in statements such as: 'I'm going to see my aunty tomorrow'. This is an area of learning which is very much concerned with real life and links to Understanding the World are obvious – furthermore when there is meaning and purpose for children they recognise that maths makes sense.

Figure 9.1 Dolphin by four-year-old girl in child-initiated activity

Experiences to support Shape, Space and Measures

Involving measure, size and distance

- Everyday activities indoors and out of doors including those – for example on bikes – when questions about distance can be asked and explored; climbing when perspective taking shows a different view of, for example, a den – when the rectangular roof is the most evident feature; building with large blocks – when structures are built after investigating buildings, foundations and stability.

Identifying shapes

- Jigsaws and form boards with pieces which fit together provide opportunities for discussion of ideas and introduction of vocabulary such as 'match', 'the same', 'bigger', 'smaller', 'different' and so on.
- Games and 'Apps' on some PCs and tablets focusing on fitting items together might include 2, 3 and 4 piece puzzles to create a picture of an animal or an apple, and those focused on helping children to recognise and identify shapes such as a triangular road sign or a plate.

Matching shapes/size for a purpose, capacity and weight

- Identifying a piece of material in the outdoor/indoor areas that will be effective in covering the floor of a den.
- Filling and emptying containers with different materials such as water, sand or rice and comparing heavier and lighter quantities.
- Ordering a series of objects – such as skittles in a row; largest to smallest of Troika type dolls that fit inside one another, or putting smaller pans inside bigger pans in home play.

Developing positional language

- Playing hide and seek and commenting on whether a child hid 'under', 'beside', 'next to', 'in front of' or 'behind' something.
- Play with road mats and cars, farm animals and pens; planting and weeding a garden.
- Play with sand, fibre and other materials which allow items to be hidden.
- Treasure hunts where children follow directions to arrive at an end point such as following a giant's footprints.
- Encouraging children during a short period of time to see how far they can throw a ball; jump horizontally, or select logs to walk over to reach a specific point, and working out which was their 'best' effort.

Familiarity with money; one to one correspondence

- Playing 'shop' with resources which invite children to handle coins, use a balance or fit items into a box or a bag.
- Shopping for real items such as straw for the guinea pigs or categorising and counting money collected for a charity.

Seriation and making patterns

- Making patterns with objects found in the outdoor or indoor areas.
- Making patterns with items such as coloured paper, shiny glass beads, Post-it Notes and other easily manipulated items.
- Lining items up from largest to smallest, heaviest to lightest.
- Movement activities that focus on use of space – use of positional language can lead to discussions of shapes such as when everybody is standing in a circle; spreading the body to take up space and retracting it to curl up in a ball.
- Symmetry – the wings of a butterfly or mirror painting.

The next chapter focuses on Understanding the World.

10 Understanding the world

Understanding the World is concerned with developing children's awareness of the world around them, their connection to it and with different people, communities and places. The way this is presented in the EYFS is through focusing on people, places, the environment and technology in three aspects, visually:

- **The World:** focuses on nature and the environment, and the things children see or learn about within these areas such as plants and animals, items that have been made, structures such as buildings, and so on.
- **People and communities:** this aspect is intended to support children's sense of identity, helping them to recognise themselves as members of families who together with other families make up the community. Through this aspect young children are supported to develop a sense of time; through hearing stories and seeing pictures and objects which have meaning for them and their families; by encouraging them to connect their own lives with those of other family and community members, and significant past and present events, and with people and places.
- **Technology:** focuses on the use of everyday objects which contain technology, including interactive toys, games, whiteboards, sound recorders, tablets, iPods, iPads, and other devices such as cameras.

Whilst these areas are presented under separate headings, in reality children learn about all of them simultaneously – beginning at home with their families and friends then extending to experiences in the wider community. Knowing the story of their own lives helps children to recognise that individuals have some shared experiences as well as ones which are unique. And, by finding out about their own family or community children begin to learn about how their family is both different from and similar to others. This area of learning, together with PSED is important for learning about diversity and difference as well as the environment and social justice. Whilst the aspect of technology is treated as a distinct strand of learning this should not be seen as separate because it has become a fundamental part of children's lives in the twenty-first century through its reach across almost every domain of life.

The learning requirement for this area states:

> **Understanding the world** involves guiding children to make sense of their physical world and their community through opportunities to explore, observe and find out about people, places, technology and the environment.
>
> (DfE, 2012: 5)

In a discussion of how children learn the Early Learning and Development Guidelines for Washington State propose: '*Children build their identities from the people, communities and places in their lives*' (Washington State, 2012: 5). It is therefore important to recognise that through learning about Understanding the World children are finding out about how to contribute to building their world. The way this is achieved will be different for every child in every community; however the particular ideas they encounter and the skills and attitudes that they develop will influence their orientation to others and the environment throughout their whole lives.

Understanding the World is different for children of different ages and at different developmental stages. A helpful way of thinking about this area is to reflect on the extent of a child's world relative to their age/stage of development, beginning with people the young child knows, the places they visit and the events that happen in their lives which will mainly be centred around the family. Next, consider how experiences of people, places and events widen out as children of three, four or five years of age take part in an increasing number of events. As children mature, they are trying hard to understand the world and the things within it – and it is through discussions about what is and what might be that helps them learn attitudes about caring for themselves, others, the environment and living things.

Children are extremely curious about everything in their environment and the focus in early childhood should be to develop their understanding of things that occur naturally such as the seasons and the life cycle as well as those things that occur because of human activity including technology. Many children are fascinated by space and children's interests in areas such as this can lead into activities and experiences that support enquiry learning. Pedagogy should then focus on helping them to develop broad skills which encourage enquiry, for example beginning by talking with children and documenting what they already know about space and space travel can provide starting points for developing provision – and for identifying what children want to know more about. This can be supported by information from a range of sources including the Internet – sites, such as www.spacekids.co.uk provide simple accessible information including key events in space history; the names of the astronauts who have walked on the moon and answers to questions such as 'What do astronauts eat?' Enquiry learning is developed when children have new information to develop their ideas, opportunities for extended play through continuous provision (in and out of doors), resources such as moon boots, suits or helmets and items to hand to aid the building of a 'moon buggy' or a 'rocket'; or for scrutiny of distant objects (a telescope) and practitioners who sensitively engage with them in sustained shared thinking.

The World

Babies try to make sense of their physical world in the womb, responding to stimulation from the outside world such as music; after birth this desire to engage with the world is built on through encounters with people and objects and phenomena such as light and sound and the taste of food. Helping young children come to an understanding of the physical world derives from encouraging them to explore the world with all their senses. A recent review of research related to the importance of access to nature for young children showed the benefits of even a *'small patch of trees on marginal urban land'* (Chawla, 2012: 48). Considering the importance of natural environments the writer, an environmental psychologist, identified that *'walking in a park, or even looking at pictures of natural landscapes, has been shown to lower heart rates, blood pressure and stress levels'* (in adults – and), *'When children are asked to draw things they would like to see in their environment it appears to be a universal tendency – from the stone cities of Lebanon to the South African veld – for them to draw trees, plants, wildlife and water'* (ibid.: 48). Amongst the many benefits cited in this review of research are those which link to impulse control, connectedness with others and the environment and greater cooperation. Importantly these are promoted through activities such as digging soil, caring for or owning animals and playing in, or simply being in, natural environments.

Creating environments which allow for these pursuits may seem impossible however imagination and creativity on the part of practitioners, as well as listening to young children, can mean that spaces can be developed which offer children a chance to experience the joy of wallowing in mud or diving into layers of damp leaves. Claire Warden, an educational consultant, describes how nursery children, when asked to describe what they would want to do out of doors, told her: *'playing in the mud, hiding where no one can see us, running down a hill, and just lying in the hammock sleeping'* (Warden,

2010: 104). The elements are very significant in children's lives since the weather shapes almost everything from what they will wear to what they will eat – observing the clouds can be both practical in that children can learn to recognise whether they bring rain or hide the sun at the same time as being a source for developing imagination when they ponder whether what they are seeing is really a dragon flicking out his tongue, or a lion with its mouth wide open ready to eat them. The natural word is more fascinating to children than many adults imagine since they have often left behind their own interest in the sticks, stones and pebbles which a child triumphantly collects whilst out walking or the feathers, bits of bark and leaves that become 'treasures' to children who encounter nature at the park.

Effective practice

Experiences that support this area for younger children include having first hand opportunities to safely explore aspects of the natural environment and plants and animals, augmented by sharing books, models or photographs and through an adult narrating the event or sharing photographs subsequently. The following are examples of experiences to support babies in the area of The World:

- Exploring how grass, water and sand feel and what happens if these are squeezed, poured or pulled.
- Experiencing how different substances behave such as bubbles, non-toxic paint, snow and water.
- Looking at and touching flowers and grasses, noticing the smell of different plants such as thornless roses and herbs.
- Observing animals and noticing differences between them – through hearing the sounds they make and watching how they move and talking about what they eat.
- Walking or riding on different surfaces which are bumpy, smooth or steep.
- Climbing and sliding down small hills and playing roly poly.
- Learning about how we care for animals by throwing bread to the birds or feeding carrots to the rabbit.

Older children will continue to be interested in explorations of the type suggested above but will develop an increasing awareness of the environment and nature through outdoor explorations in the setting as well as outings in the locality where they might see wildlife such as geese, horses or cows and experience being in larger spaces that safely allow them to explore terrain with hills, sand or mud and find items such as stones, acorns and conkers.

Supporting children's interests in scientific thinking links to both the natural and built environment – questions focusing on 'why', 'how' and 'what if' are suggested in New York State Guidelines (The NY State Dept., 2011/12) to consider principles such as floating and sinking, and properties of objects as well as differences between different items – for example a piece of balsa wood which is light compared with a piece of bogwood which is extremely heavy and saturated with water even though it feels dry to the touch.

In addition to focusing on the earth children are also interested in the sky above as well as in all sorts of living things that they encounter (in reality, as well as in books and in other media); these may be as diverse as shells, worms, ants, beetles, dinosaurs, extra-terrestrial creatures and space travel and so on. Helping children to develop and maintain this interest is achieved through skilful pedagogy referred to earlier. Referring to the examples of effective pedagogy in Figure 5.3 consider the types of provision, experiences and interactions which may have led to the scenarios in Table 10.1 in the column headed: 'What the child might say or do'; then consider how adults might interact with children, or what further experiences or resources might be offered to scaffold their learning further in relation to each.

People and Communities

The community is made up of people who live or work in a particular area and might be experienced by a young child as a series of hubs, or webs of relationships, as indicated in Figure 10.1.

As children mature and, depending on family circumstances, their experiences of being members of a particular community widen to include other people and communities and may involve sharing in specific activities as well as celebrations and religious or cultural events. Building on from children's own experiences requires careful consideration of what the child is familiar with, what may be new or strange to the child and how to engage the child in finding out about their own lives and the lives of people they know and the environment, including technology.

Attitudes as well as knowledge are importantly learned through this aspect which supports children to gain an insight into their own lives and those of others. Tolerance, for example, derives from being understood, listened to and accepted, whilst acceptance of others springs from developing a sense of belonging in a family and a community where one is cared for. These habits should be nurtured by caregivers who 'see' the world from the child's perspective, recognising that in order to make sense of their experiences they need time to process new encounters with the world alongside adult

Table 10.1 Understanding the World: Linked to The World and Technology Using Scientific Skills drawn from The New York State Education Department (2012) Prekindergarten Foundation for the Common Core, Albany, New York

What the Child Might Say or Do	UW: The World and Technology	Identify Interactions, Further Experiences or Resources to Enhance Child's Learning
'We planted two seeds but only one has grown – I think the other one is getting ready to grow'.	Child asking and answering questions and making predictions about what they observe.	
Physically pressing a teddy bear's tummy to hear it make a sound; or using a mouse on a PC whilst playing a game to press an arrow which keeps a teddy bear in the middle of a plank balanced on a tub.	Child manipulating objects to understand what they are like.	
Noticing that it is sunny and then when it rains discussing causes such as: 'cos the clouds have come across the sky'.	Child talking about what they see and noticing when things change.	
Trying to pull open a bag of carrot sticks singlehandedly; realising that won't work and asking another child to hold one side so that they can do it together; or getting scissors to cut the packet open, or asking somebody stronger to open it.	Child trying different approaches to solving problems they encounter in daily life.	

'I think the balloon will float away because it's full of air' or 'I think the boat will sink because the load is too heavy.'	Child predicting what might happen and explaining reasoning.
The child may notice a butterfly has landed on a bush and chooses to photograph it to get a better view of it or to look at it through a magnifying glass.	Child uses a magnifying glass or other tools to enhance observation or to record what they have seen.
The child may notice that the dens children have made in the outdoor area are constructed with different materials or are shaped differently.	Child compares different things they have seen.
The child might share photographs they have taken of all the different natural items they used to make a pattern in the veranda area.	Child talks about or represents some of the things they have observed.
The child may look at images of space in a range of fiction (such as *Whatever Next, Murphy*, 2007) and in non-fiction books, and photographs in electronic formats.	Child may be interested in outer space and exploration of space and shows an interest in knowing about the moon and stars.

(Continued)

Table 10.1 (*Continued*)

What the Child Might Say or Do	UW: The World and Technology	Identify Interactions, Further Experiences or Resources to Enhance Child's Learning
The child may compare sizes, colours and other distinguishing features of dog breeds and may enjoy looking at books, pictures or stories about different dogs, comparing with their own pet dog at home.	Child wants to find out about different dog breeds.	
The child may dig in different (undesignated) places; or want to make a 'map' showing different surfaces such as sand, wood, concrete and so on.	Child investigates different surfaces inside and outside.	
The child may hit a rattle repeatedly to hear a sound; or throw a ball to knock down light plastic bottles which rattle when they fall over.	Child is interested in cause and effect.	
A younger child might pull bits of fresh orange out their cup when they notice them at the bottom; or an older child may squeeze oranges and use different items to sieve the 'bits' out.	Child is interested in finding out about the properties of liquids/solids and how these can be changed.	

A younger child may push a car along a road mat; an older child may introduce a slope and apply friction to make a car go fast.	Child is interested in position of objects and learning about the use of different spaces in the environment; child is interested in movement and force.
The child mixes water and sand together or enjoys baking or making dough or milkshake.	Child is fascinated by 'mixing' solids and liquids and observing changes
The child may be very interested in trying to hammer nails into different surfaces such as soft wood, hard wood, chipboard or polystyrene.	Child experiments with tools such as a hammer which is used to find out what items can be joined successfully.

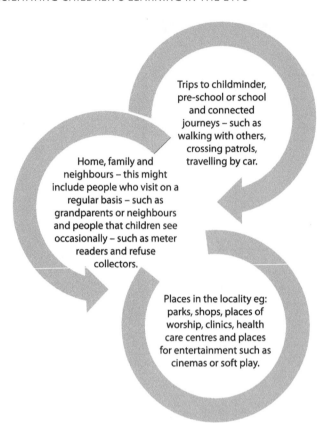

Figure 10.1 Community for the child represented as area hubs and webs of relationships

guides who help them to interpret their experiences and inspire them to find out more.

Effective practice

Most settings support children to develop a sense of belonging through communicating with children and their families and encouraging children to share experiences of events in their lives; both significant 'big' events like their own birthday as well as 'small' events such as the child being collected by 'grandma' at the end of the day. Recalling and reminiscing about events that happened in the past supports young children's ability to remember events as well as to develop a personal narrative supporting their sense of identity. Sensitively discussing different experiences supports children to feel confident about their own individuality and that of the family and community they belong to. Many settings draw on a community with shared culture and ethnicity; others are more diverse and children have the opportunity to hear many distinctive languages and witness various customs and cultural practices. Making sense of these differences is interpreted in New Zealand's Early Years Curriculum: Te Whāriki, which identifies the following knowledge, skills and attitudes that children develop through this aspect of learning:

- *'An understanding of their own rights and those of others*
- *The ability to recognise discriminatory practices and behaviour and to respond appropriately*
- *Some early concepts of the value of appreciating diversity and fairness*
- *The self-confidence to stand up for themselves and others against biased ideas and discriminatory behaviour*
- *Positive judgements on their own gender and the opposite gender*
- *Positive judgements on their own ethnic group and other ethnic groups*
- *Confidence that their family background is viewed positively within the early childhood setting*
- *Respect for children who are different from themselves and ease of interaction with them.'* (NZ Ministry of Education, 1996: 66).

The accompanying reflective questions offered for discussion in respect of these support the outcome for this aspect set out in the explanatory note to the ELG: People and Communities: *'They* [children] *listen, comment and show sensitivity towards other children's experiences, communities and traditions which may be the same or different to their own'* (STA, 2012: 29). Questions from Te Whāriki include:

- *'What do adults do when children are excluded by others and what effects do adults' actions have?*
- *How do all adults challenge negative and stereotyped language and attitudes and what impact does this have?*
- *How are books and pictures selected, and do these procedures ensure that books and pictures show children of different gender, ethnicity, age, and ability in a range of roles?'* (NZ Ministry of Education, 1996: 66).

Finding the answers to 'how' and 'why' questions helps children to learn about their own history, their family's history and about the community where they live. Referring to the examples of effective pedagogy in Figure 5.3 consider the types of provision, experiences and interactions which may have led to the scenarios in Table 10.2 in the column headed: 'What the child might say or do'; then consider how adults might interact with children or

Table 10.2 Developing children's interests in Understanding the World through: People and communities and technology

What the Child Might Say or Do	UW: People and Communities and Technology	Identify Interactions, Further Experiences or Resources to Enhance Child's Learning
A young child may be fascinated by mirrors and look at their own image or reach out to touch other children's faces; an older child might compare pictures of their younger self with their present self.	Child is finding out about themselves and others through exploring similarities and differences relating to what they are like; what they can do; what they used to be like.	
A child might anticipate an event because the 'tidy time' song is started.	Child is identifying what will happen next based on previous experience.	
A child talks about something they have done the day before or refers to an earlier event by pointing to a sign.	Child is developing an awareness of time through recalling past events that are important to them.	
A child role plays roles of community members such as a member of the police or a builder.	Child is gaining an understanding of the community in which they live and of different roles within it.	
A child is using an iPod to take a photograph of their friends.	Child is selecting technology for a particular purpose and using it to record an event.	

A toddler presses buttons that make a sound on a toy mobile which he then puts to his ear before saying: 'Hello'.	Child is learning to operate a toy which has a microchip and recognises how technology is used.
A young child might get excited looking at pictures or book about family members; an older child might notice a picture in a book of an elderly person with a walking stick and might say: 'That's like my grandad'.	Child is learning about differences between people
A child might bring food to share related to a particular festival in the community or to celebrate an occasion such as their birthday.	Child is developing an understanding of what is important and distinctive about their own community.
A child might be invited to a party at their friend's house and agree to attend even though they may be anxious about the prospect.	Child is learning to be sensitive to the needs of others, recognising their attendance at a celebration is important.
A child may understand several languages and use different ones appropriately when they wish to communicate with others.	Child is developing confidence in themselves and knows about differences between themselves and others.
A child talks about 'seeing' distant relatives on the PC.	Child is developing an understanding that electronic communication connects people through programmes such as Skype or other means.

what experiences or resources might be offered to scaffold their learning further in relation to each.

Technology

Advances in technology over the last two decades have been phenomenal and continue to both engage and challenge many adults as well as children. Activities such as electronic communication through social networking, texting and emailing have reached record levels and the uses of technology in many systems cannot fail to impact children's lives. However, as the National Association for the Education of Young Children (NAEYC) indicates young children's experiences with and use of technology should be considered carefully, since: *'For technology to be developmentally appropriate, it should be responsive to the ages and developmental levels of the children, to their individual needs and interests, and to their social and cultural contexts'* (Dale McManis and Gunnewig, 2012: 16). So a major consideration in introducing children to technology is its appropriateness relative to the child's social and cultural experiences as well as in relation to their age or stage of development. *Development Matters* provides brief suggestions about this area in respect of children up to the age of three and slightly more information in respect of children from 30–50 months. That this information is brief may be indicative of the fact that opinions about young children's use of technology vary considerably – many arguing that in the first two years children should not be exposed to electronic media including television, DVDs and so on. Though it would seem that this group may be reducing since, according to a recent policy statement from the American Academy of Paediatrics, an organisation dedicated to the health of all children, *'90% of parents report that their children younger than 2 watch some form of electronic media'* (American Academy of Pediatrics, 2011: 1); whilst by three years of age some one third of children have television sets in their bedrooms. However providing appropriate support for children who use the range of media including the Internet, smartphones, tablets and related technology must be a priority involving safety procedures as well as those which guide children to experiences which are valuable, rather than time-filling. When this is achieved even young children have been seen to benefit; for example, in a study of the use of iPads by two to eight year olds findings showed that children as young as two years of age can use 'Apps' which are meaningful to them since touch screen technology provides easy access and, provided the App is at the appropriate level developmentally for the child, can be engaging and has some value in other areas of learning, for example, problem solving (Michael Cohen Group LLC, 2011). Another analysis of recent research (Dale McManis and Gunnewig, 2012: 16) showed positive outcomes for children's learning when adults were involved in mentoring and guiding them in use of such media; reported benefits included:

- Increases in young children's cognitive, and literacy skills
- Increases in interactions with peers around computer use
- Gains in abstract reasoning, planning behaviour, visual-motor coordination and visual memory
- Better outcomes in language and literacy including letter recognition, comprehension and listening and understanding of story concepts
- Increased mathematical understanding – including numbers and shapes (ibid.).

Clearly as increasing focus is placed on integrating technological tools into early childhood education more research will emerge supporting current understanding of the role of technology in their learning, however, it is important to recognise that like every resource the potential value of any piece of equipment is linked to how it is used, rather than to what it is.

Research undertaken in Scotland into three and four year old children's use of technology at home confirms the importance of parental partnership since it revealed that whilst children experienced a range of technology in the home it did not dominate or hinder social interaction and asserted that '*By understanding more about how children experience technologies in the home context, educators are more likely to be able to incorporate them into the early years setting and recognise the extended repertoire of skills, dispositions and competences that are possible*' (Plowman *et al.*, 2012: 5). These may include '*making a picture, playing a game, recording a story, taking a photo or making a book, or engaging in other age-appropriate learning activities*' (NAEYC, 2012: 6); and might include combining a number of skills such as recording their own learning journey by recording stages in a process such as making a model – beginning by photographing the items used; then talking about the steps involved – such as fixing wheels and finally showing the finished product – this could then be developed with the practitioner to display the information so that another child could learn about what to do if they wanted to make a similar model. The skill of the practitioner is in ensuring that children's learning is supported and extended through demonstrating some of the approaches discussed previously, such as modelling. Ultimately children learn what is modelled and if small incidents such as finding a spider in the corner of a room are seen as opportunities for learning then time will be given to important considerations such as where the spider came from, how the spider might be caught and remain unharmed and finding a suitable place to put the spider when it is finally caught. On the other hand if encounters such as this are seen as barriers to learning something more important then children may consider that the area of Understanding the World is less so. Additional information about Understanding the World is set out in *Development Matters* which provides useful ideas to support this area further.

The next chapter addresses Expressive Arts and Design.

11 Expressive arts and design

This area of learning focuses on children's creativity in the arts and ways of representing their own ideas, thoughts and feelings. However in order to be able to represent their ideas children need to see and experience different forms of art including visual, dramatic and performance arts. Discussing the importance of the arts in early education an arts advocacy group argues the 'added value' of this area of learning, stating: *'Basic literacy, numeracy and scientific concepts are introduced through music, movement and visual arts making. Social skills important for tolerance, understanding and celebration of diversity, are developed through arts experiences such as dramatic play, singing and dancing'* (Meiners, 2008: 1).

However the place of Expressive Arts and Design (EAD) in the EYFS (2012) also demonstrates a recognition that the arts are important in themselves, in addition to the benefits they may bring to other areas of children's learning and development. EAD requires that children have opportunities to explore and engage with experiences and resources related to:

- Design and technology
- Art
- Music
- Dance
- Role play
- Stories

These areas are referred to in the following interconnected aspects of EAD:

- Exploring and Using Media and Materials
- Being Imaginative

As well as creating opportunities for children to engage in finding out about, creating and responding to design and technology, art, music, dance, role

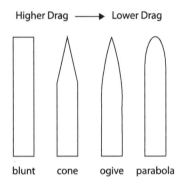

Figure 11.1 Image for rocket shape

play and stories, extended periods should be set aside so that children have sufficient opportunities to pursue their interests. In addition adults should be on hand when this takes place since children frequently require their support in problem-solving and to extend their ideas. Imagine, for example, a five year old applying their skills to make a space rocket; they may need help to consider what shape of object will best serve their plan – reference to books, photographs and images from NASA or a safe image resource bank may influence their choice since the 'nose' of a rocket might be an important feature the child is aware of but is not necessarily able to explain. The images below sourced at Google show there to be different 'rocket shapes' affecting propulsion which the child may consider together with the materials available; pedagogy might focus on helping the child to think about how to modify a blunt ended object such as a cylinder by the addition of a cone shape to make a more aerodynamic model. Testing different 'nose' shapes (Figure 11.1) by adding shuttlecocks of different materials and construction, including home-made corks with feathers attached, may then lead into other areas of learning or satisfy a child's trajectory schema – an interest in throwing or projecting objects.

The child may then want to fix together different pieces to construct their rocket and may need an adult to scaffold their thinking, helping them identify (a) what needs to be done and (b) possible fixing methods, to use. Sometimes teaching a child skills at a particular moment may be necessary in order to create an effect the child is seeking; for example how to join the selected cylinder to the nose. The adult may begin by showing the child a method of preparation using small incisions to nick the top of the cylinder creating 'joined curving'; which after glue or another fixer is used will allow the flat surface to join with the cylinder, as shown in Figure 11.2:

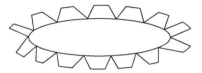

Figure 11.2 Joined curving to fix a cylinder to a surface

As the child's rocket begins to emerge they may wish to create a metallic effect to the body by the addition of holographic paper or stickers or foil. This may lead into considerations of whether a person will take the rocket into orbit and whether they will need special clothing, food and so on, which in turn might become a narrative in which the child is either the story teller or the astronaut taking their craft into space. Therefore the boundaries of the areas listed above should not be restricted since for a young child the horizons of creativity overlap, blend and diffuse into many colours, textures and 'languages'. A key aspect of teaching EAD in the early years is to maintain children's self-belief whilst encouraging their reflexivity about their own processes and their ingress into different art forms. Bernadette Duffy OBE, head of the Coram Early Years Centre where creativity and the arts are seen as important in the lives of young children reminds that: '*Through the arts children can comprehend, respond to, and represent their perceptions. They can develop their understanding of the world, experience beauty and express their cultural heritage. Such experiences help children to gain self-esteem and create a view of the world that is uniquely their own*' (Duffy, 2010: 25).

Duffy writes about the challenge of being the supporter of design, art, music, movement and the dramatic arts in a discussion of a music project, 'Finding Our Voices', which the centre engaged with:

> *As a staff team we were aware that music making was an area in which many of us lacked confidence and we needed an experienced music maker to support our own musical development alongside that of the children. We wanted music to be embedded into the life of the centre, not to be something a music teacher does once a week with the children.*
>
> (Ibid.: 25)

The opportunity for engaging with this project, however, was recognised as valuable because practitioners believed '*musicality is an innate human characteristic and that involvement in music making not only gives children a chance to develop musical concepts and skills but also encourages self-esteem and well-being*' (ibid.: 24).

As the project progressed Duffy reported:

> *Children, parents and staff attend regular music sessions with the music maker and as staff confidence develops they take over the sessions with the support of the music maker. The sessions are linked to the on-going work of the centre and the songs and music from the sessions become part of its day-to-day life. The children also have the opportunity to listen to and work with visiting musicians from a range of musical traditions and to share their music making with their parents and the wider community.*
>
> (Ibid.: 25)

When choices are made about whether continuing professional development for practitioners should focus on literacy or EAD it is unlikely in the short term that spending will be directed towards the arts – this is clearly a concern. Therefore making the most of the skills of those talented in these areas within settings is likely to be a priority so that children can benefit from observing and interacting with them. In addition, there are story tellers, artists, musicians, actors and dancers in many communities and therefore engaging with community projects can either bring access to budding or established artists, willing to share their expertise, or to small amounts of funding for projects.

Other useful connections to support arts development could include a local brass band, Caribbean band, or orchestra. The Halle Orchestra, and no doubt other city orchestras, are occasionally funded to work with young children in schools on arts projects in which, through links with musicians from a section of the orchestra, children are assisted to explore ways of dramatising stories and becoming familiar with different forms of music.

Dramatisations, narratives and role play are all aspects of pretence or imaginary play which most children readily engage in from as early as 18 months of age. These may range from instances such as 'dancing' in imitation of characters seen on TV to pretending to be an animal. Through such activities children connect ideas in order to make sense of experiences or events in their lives – sometimes these may be major – such as having experienced a frightening event like thinking they are lost; or minor – such as observing how a cat laps its milk.

Initially imaginary experiences may remain within the child yet research shows that as slightly older children engage with one another in *'Activities such as dramatic play or dancing in unison'* they enter a domain where *'collaboration and cooperation skills such as group singing, dancing and dramatic play'* require *'sharing, taking turns, and subordinating individual urges to the intentions of the group'* (Brouillette, 2010: 18). Again this area should not be considered in isolation from either the creative process or from the strands of EAD referred to at the start of this chapter since spontaneous play is unpredictable and whilst a child's explorations may begin in one place they may well end in a very different place. For example, I recently learned about a group of children fascinated by a cocoon they had found in the nursery garden, who were curious to know where it came from and why it was in a particular place. Supporting such an entrée into following children's interests the following strategies are proposed by writers whose work in this area was discussed in a review of research undertaken for the Arts Council in 2001 and 2004:

- *'Asking open-ended questions*
- *Tolerating ambiguity*
- *Modelling creative thinking and behaviour*
- *Encouraging experimentation and persistence*
- *Praising children who find unexpected answers'* (Sharp, 2004: 7).

An example of the 'learning journey' children had encountered in the nursery included: consideration of the life cycle of the cocoon from egg through to butterfly – enhanced by the provision of fiction and non-fiction books; close observations of the cocoon and representations of the life cycle of the emerging creature from curled up egg, wrapped cocoon and ground-hugging caterpillar to gossamer-winged butterfly. Further explorations included mark-making and drawing and encounters with movement, sound and music.

Art in early childhood settings is sometimes limited by resources or limited specialist knowledge of a particular art form by practitioners who may fear 'wasting money' on a resource they are not confident to use, such as clay which is expensive, and needs to be taken care of if it is to last long enough to be considered an economical resource. Yet, as teacher educators researching practice in early childhood settings suggest: *'For young children art has great meaning. The artwork of a child is an extension of him/her as a human being'* (Twigg and Garvis, 2010: 199). Therefore as educators valuing children's art is as important as being non-judgemental about what is 'good'; though this does not mean that skills and attitudes should not be taught which encourage children to think about what they have seen, or how they have executed a particular piece and how they might wish to extend or add to work or create it in a different medium.

Returning to the cocoon scenario described above, the teacher reported that a four year old in her group had returned to the computer on three different days to develop her butterfly picture complete with symmetrical wing markings. Interestingly, she had used only one colour, focusing on pattern, which may have been influenced by other art experiences offered in the learning environment such as the images placed next to dry sand where photographs invited the children to make 'zig zags', 'circles', 'stripes', 'words' and 'swirls' in sand.

The New Zealand Early Childhood Curriculum, Te Whāriki, addresses many of the areas of EAD describing them as goals for Communication, specifically: *'Children experience an environment where they discover and develop different ways to be creative and expressive'* (NZ Ministry of Education, 1996: 72), in effect this is what the intention is behind the outcomes for EAD in the EYFS. However the details of this journey are limited in respect of babies from birth to 11 months, though more information is provided in *Development Matters* for children in the older age range. The following examples of experiences and activities that focus on this area of learning for babies up to one year might therefore be helpful in planning to support babies' development in EAD:

Table 11.1 Supporting babies' EAD

What the Child Might Communicate or Do	EAD: Exploring and Using Media and Materials and Being Imaginative
Turning or stopping on hearing sounds or noticing movement (both in and out of doors).	Child is finding out about sources of sound and light, patterns, colours.
Mouthing objects or reaching out to touch or hold an object.	Child is exploring properties of objects involving texture and shape and how materials respond to their actions – for example the child may be working out whether something is soft or firm.
Grasping and squeezing items on a mat containing different (safe) fixed materials such as metal or wooden rings, satin ribbons and so on.	Child is experimenting with materials and objects to find out how they feel, such as for example if they are smooth, rough, cold or malleable.
Jigging or bouncing to music, playing with sounds and babbling.	Child is listening and responding to music and may move to rhythm and beat, preferring some tempos to others.
Clapping, banging on a surface such as a table.	Child is exploring sound sources and patterns of sounds.
Placing hands or fingers in paint, gloop, liquids, sand or leaves.	Child is exploring how different materials, including media such as paint, act or can be changed or transformed in some way.

Looking at a picture book and reaching out to an image of a woolly lamb, for example, with excitement.	Child is responding emotionally to a pleasing image and may endeavour to grasp or pull picture.
Hugging a teddy bear, soft toy or transitional object such as a sheet, or cuddle blanket.	Child may be using the object to symbolise a loved one; responding through connecting with the object affectionately.

Providing an interesting and exciting array of materials and resources to support this area of learning is important however to augment commercially sourced items clean recycled materials sourced locally and through the community can provide any amount of suitable materials. Whether these are offered in areas of provision or workshops dedicated to specific aspects of EAD or in an EAD area they should be supplemented by writing materials as well as a range of books and pictures to arouse a child's curiosity about new areas of interest.

Art

The focus of art at this stage is encouraging children to explore colour and texture and to satisfy their desire to represent their thoughts, ideas and feelings. Finding out about colour requires that children are given the freedom to explore, by mixing and using media such as paint in ways that are satisfying – this may occur in or out of doors. The following resources should be available if at all possible, bearing in mind the developmental stage of children in the group:

- Brushes ranging from stubby to slim in thickness some of which are capable of covering large areas such as a canvas fixed to an outer wall, and those that might be required to paint a line to indicate brickwork on a house painted on a piece of A3 paper.
- Paper of different thicknesses and textures, including patterned and printed paper, this might be used for tearing and creating collages or for decorating a den for a dragon.
- Sponges of various sizes and textures (close and open) for use in mixing paint, taking off paint from brushes and printing.
- Pots for adding water to dry paint and rinsing brushes.
- Different types of paint to allow for individual exploration of an idea – this might include tempera paint to scrape on and off strong paper using a trowel or similar object; acrylic and watercolour paint

as well as the usual powder and ready mixed varieties sometimes enhanced with the addition of washing liquid and by blowing into the mixture with a drinking straw to make bubble prints, or combining inks and oils to create marbling effects.

- Materials to cut up, shred, tear or shape to add to pictures or backgrounds the child creates should also be available – out of doors these might include natural materials such as stones, shells, leaves, conkers, twigs, fir cones, walnut shells, sea urchins, dried seeds and acorns; indoors these could include sequins, shiny and matt materials such as small pieces of plastic sheeting, pieces of lightweight vinyl flooring; buttons, bottle tops, corks, wool, string and any number of items found in everyday use.

- The addition of beautifully displayed pictures and visuals created by other children, other artists and themselves help children to recognise that their efforts are valued pieces of art, it also makes exploration of this area irresistible to young children who seem almost to need the satisfaction of applying layer after layer of paint.

- Babies do not require the same range of tools and equipment as toddlers or older children because they may simply find out about paint or other viscous fluids, such as gloop, through touching, feeling and literally exploring them with the whole of the upper body; some settings encourage babies to use their whole body to explore paint, for example.

Designing and making

- Many settings provide a 'making' area alongside art resources so that children can access and use them at will.

- A space with room for designing and drawing models as well as for making things is important.

- Materials, including boxes, small dowelling rods, and smooth wood offcuts, card, paper clips, Sellotape, PVA glue, tubes, bottle tops, string, foil, scissors and writing tools should be effective for the 'job' in hand.

- Skills such as rolling paper or ribbon to make it curl up need to be taught.

- When a good range of materials is available and children can find what they need to create a boat or a car they experience a sense of satisfaction because they have created something from their own ideas.

- Babies and toddlers explore materials by examining them to find out what they feel like either to touch or when handled; manipulating items for long periods to explore them; dropping one item in favour of another and placing items into one another.

Malleable materials

- Another staple provision in most settings is an area where children can create with dough, clay, gloop and other malleable materials.
- Providing resources to support exploration of the properties of these materials can extend children's interests in manipulating and making items such as pretend food or other artefacts.
- These materials offer a range of open-ended resources and opportunities for the development of small motor skills, language, creativity and imagination.
- Enhanced by the addition of pictures and visual prompts these materials can be transported easily in tiny tubs and cement trays dependent on children's agendas and what is available.

ICT and EAD

- With the rapid increase in mobile technology such as iPods, iPads and tablets, light boxes as well as more traditional devices, such as laptops and more permanent ICT equipment such as interactive whiteboards, projectors and photocopiers, opportunities of various kinds can be created to integrate use of these items into the EAD curriculum.
- Most of the above can be used to create and make pictures, to develop narrated stories, illustrated either with pictures or photographs created by children and to explore mark-making of various kinds to create images and artefacts that children enjoy. See Figures 11.3 and 11.4:

Figure 11.3 A Monster in Forest produced independently by a four-year-old using a PC and mouse

Figure 11.4 A Rotational Schema explored with a pen on an IWB by a three-year-old boy

Music and movement

- Music and movement areas are sometimes developed for organisational purposes yet many resources may be incorporated into role play or story telling or taught sessions.
- A wide range of resources can be provided for making untuned instruments such as shakers and box guitars.
- Provision of commercially made instruments alongside these may include percussion instruments, for example, triangles, tambourines, cymbals, gongs or cow bells.
- Besides exploring rhythm and beat there should be opportunities for children to listen to world music and for singing and movement.
- A range of scarves, ribbons and other items can encourage children's interest in moving to music, and CDs and voice recorders or microphones can encourage listening and singing.
- Recent research evidence shows that *'music education during childhood, even in limited form, may influence the adult brain'* ... reinforcing *'the proposition that music is an agent of positive, experience-dependent plasticity'*, in other words by introducing children to musical instruction new neural connections are formed and it is now known that *'past musical experience is predictive of enhanced cognitive performance in older adults'* (Skoe and Krauss, 2012: 11509) – good reasons for supporting development in this area.

Imaginative play

- Imaginative play is linked to symbolic representation and is important because it supports children's thinking as well as their ability to understand that one thing can 'stand' for another – a feature of writing and reading – that symbols represent sounds and words.
- Children's imaginative play can take place anywhere and is not restricted to particular areas or spaces so it is just as likely that imaginative play will take place outside in the sand pit or in a book area.
- Amongst the most frequently found opportunities for imaginative play in early childhood settings is home play which offers a context for many things including connecting with home, projecting into future roles, reflecting on and coming to terms with events and inventing scenarios which are explored and revealed as the play emerges – this might happen as an antidote to commonplace play in an area where a child sees its potential for offering an inviting backdrop to the pursuits of super-hero play!
- Providing many contexts for imaginative play by adapting or diversifying basic role play to accommodate new areas of interest ensures its relevance – and, in consultation with children may become a pirate ship, a cave, an underwater scenario or something else.
- Equally, imaginative provision inspired by children's interests may include those developed to support different children's schemas or interests by extending resources to accommodate a particular interest – for example an outdoor area may be developed to create a 'car wash' area complete with hoses, buckets, leather dusters, sponges, till and money, price lists and bays for customer parking.
- Imaginative play is also often offered successfully in the provision of 'small worlds', boxes containing most of the resources necessary to create a small world, whether a polar paradise complete with penguins or a world inhabited by dinosaurs.
- The child's capacity to imagine other 'worlds' even imaginary ones will be extended through looking at books, viewing short films and through discussions with knowledgeable others, as well as first hand experiences that help connect the real world with the imaginary – for example being in a forest may support the child's imagination of a time when the world was less populated than the present.

Construction

- Wooden blocks, the 'Trojan horse' of learning, offer enormous potential to develop EAD (amongst many other areas of learning).

- Blocks might be found in a quiet corner of the indoor area or located outside in a simple wooden structure sited under sailcloth.
- An inviting area will provide exciting possibilities to children intent on designing and building structures, particularly if resources such as tape measures, clip boards and spirit levels or high visibility jackets and wheelbarrows are available.
- Block play develops in stages with sensory exploration of blocks by babies leading to placing of blocks in a small pile by toddlers.
- Transporting and piling blocks occurs during the next phase followed by an interest in the sound and movement of blocks that fall.
- When 'building' begins it is characterised by repetition with horizontal, road-like structures or vertical, tower-like structures.
- The imaginative use of blocks may begin with making a block stand for a phone; this then extends to the lined-up blocks being seen as a road.
- Increasing maturity and ability to visualise transformation of a series of blocks then leads the child to create more sophisticated structures such as an enclosure for animals or connecting a series of blocks to make an arch.
- Eventually children begin to integrate their wider knowledge of the world to create buildings of different types and to consider issues connected with balancing, symmetry and so on.
- Observing how real structures are created will increase the quality of the play as will pictures, posters and travel brochures of buildings such as the Burj-Khalifa, Dubai, the tallest building in the world.

Ultimately EAD is intended to nurture children's explorations in art, music, movement, dance, roleplay, and design and technology, in doing so children should have opportunities to do exactly that – the things which many adults fondly remember doing – exploring their own creative pursuits. When thinking about the nature of pedagogy in relation to EAD the explanatory note for both ELGs is helpful in emphasising that for the purpose of assessing this ELG:

- *Processes are more important* than the finished product which need not necessarily occur;
- *music is any generation of sound with intent* to represent an idea or feeling; and
- *dance is any form of movement* by which children express themselves, emotions or responses.
- The child may recall and sings songs independently *as he or she engages with other activities.*

- The child *creates and explores music and dance in their own way*; they experiment and change sounds and movements in their play.
- The child *uses a variety of materials, tools and techniques* safely through an exploration of colour, design, texture, form and function.

Finally, children do not doubt their own abilities in the arts – a child's disposition to exploring the arts is influenced by the nature of relationships and interactions that help them to see themselves as competent and capable – arts education is about helping each child find the artist within themselves whether that is an engineer, a musician, a writer or a sculptor – early experiences shape a child's view – positively or negatively. The following chapter considers the place of areas of learning such as EAD and UW in the EYFS, and how the EYFS may need to develop to keep pace with the inevitable changes created by technological advances and changing government priorities.

12   Teaching beyond the EYFS: A curriculum for the twenty-first century?

Discussing the role of ideas in creativity Professor Simone Ritter at the Radboud University concludes *'today's world of continuous change thrives on creative individuals and inventive organizations'* (Ritter *et al.*, 2012: 21). She and a community of scientists across the Western hemisphere are beginning to identify how so called 'light bulb moments' arise, leading to insights capable of changing the course of history and the future of humanity. Discussing these kinds of moments, a website (BBC Science, 2013) reminds the reader of the circumstances leading to earlier great discoveries beginning with Archimedes' eureka moment when he allegedly discovered the principle of buoyancy whilst bathing, and Charles Darwin, who whilst reading for pleasure formulated the theory of natural selection, and more mundanely, though nonetheless importantly, Arthur Fry who, with knowledge of a type of glue, invented by his friend, went on to create the Post-it note so that he could use it to easily return to a particular page in his hymn book. Notably women's insights are barely represented, possibly reflecting women's modesty in these matters, or their lack of contemplative time, the only one offered as Oprah Winfrey's popularisation of an 'Aha' moment – describing *'the exact realisation someone has when they need to change their life'*. However, more seriously the scientists referred to in the blog have identified the following approaches as those which support this area:

'Five ways to be more creative:

- *Do things differently*
- *Cut distractions*
- *Work on mundane tasks*
- *Just let your mind wander*
- *Don't be afraid to improvise and take risks'* (ibid.).

Reflecting on these areas reminds me of a sign I noticed in a printer's recently, which read *'Children need the freedom and time to play. Play is not a luxury.*

Play is a necessity. Whilst the words seemed familiar to me I couldn't place them or recall which educationalist might have written them, until I found the words attributed to Kay Redfield Jamison, Professor of Psychiatry at the Johns Hopkins University, Baltimore. According to Big Think (Big Think, 2013), Kay is a prominent expert on mental health issues as well as creativity and her words resonate because they represent some of the shift that Jack Shonkoff, called for in 2000 through 'From Neurons to Neighborhoods' (NRC and IOM, 2000), a seminal report into early childhood, in which his committee identified interactions among early childhood science, policy and practice as in need of dramatic rethinking. The extent to which Shonkoff's committee's aims were achieved was reassessed in 2012 when his team identified that the early childhood development community can be simultaneously proud and dissatisfied with how far it has come since its inception, arguing that whilst the first and second of the committee's aims had been achieved in promoting understanding that *'All children are born wired for feelings and ready to learn'* and that *'Early environments matter and nurturing relationships are essential'*; he felt the changing needs of young children in society still needed to be addressed as did the nature of interactions among early childhood science and policy and practice (IOM and NRC 2012: 43).

Clearly, addressing the latter concern will continue, as many different voices, from a range of disciplines contribute new knowledge to debates about early childhood – reflecting this, the words of several psychiatrists have been quoted in this publication, symptomatic of the convergence of opinions about the needs of children in the 'world of continuous change' discussed by Ritter. However, if in the future today's children are to be the 'creative individuals' in the 'inventive organizations' she refers to, in England, the EYFS curriculum must be the springboard for their creativity.

This suggests that through this period children should develop a sense of their own individuality at the same time as a recognition of their responsibilities to themselves and others; a sense of well-being and connectedness with other people and places and opportunities to explore ideas and to reflect on them, if necessary by standing back and letting their minds 'wander' as the eminent proponents of creativity have demonstrated. However, further deliberation reminds me that the five ways to be more creative describe children at play:

1   *Doing things differently* occurs when children do things such as, for no apparent reason, dropping a toy they have just selected in favour of selecting a nearby book.
2   *Cut distractions* is apparent when children concentrate to achieve their own ends, such as playing in the sink with two empty plastic bottles oblivious of the world around them.

3 *Work on mundane tasks* is evident when young children engage repeatedly in activities to some point of satisfaction (that they are rarely able to explain).

4 *Just let your mind wander* is apparent when a child is simply 'being' – either mentally, or physically.

5 *Don't be afraid to improvise and take risks* is evident when a child is undeterred by lack of a particular resource and willingly represents it by using something else – for example, a cardboard box might be used in place of a toy garage. Risk taking in this context is an indication that the child is 'in flow' and open to new experiences.

Alison Gopnik contends that babies and young children lack inhibition and that whilst this might seem to be a huge handicap, in reality it is precisely because of this that they are able to explore freely, unhindered by analytical thought or consideration of the possible consequences of their actions (ironically, adults are encouraged to develop this disposition to enhance their creativity). She suggests that the trade-off between the two: being able to explore creatively and learn flexibly, like a child, and being able to plan and act effectively, like an adult are oppositional since '*The very qualities needed to act efficiently – such as swift automatic processing and a highly pruned brain network – may be intrinsically antithetical to the qualities that are useful for learning, such as flexibility*' (Gopnik, 2010: 81). Concluding that far from being '*unfinished adults, babies and young children are exquisitely designed by evolution to change and create, to learn and explore*' (ibid.: 81), a sentiment to which anybody who has worked with young children will attest. Maintaining children's creativity and promoting their play and explorations are requirements of the EYFS, so too are the learning requirements and assessments in the EYFS. Guidance to local authorities in relation to the EYFSP indicates that all areas of learning within the EYFS are important, yet in devising a 'good level of development', in order to measure attainment nationally, the focus is on the prime areas in addition to literacy and mathematics, whilst reference to Understanding the World and Expressive Arts and Design is omitted – though these are important for children's well-being and their connection with people and the environment. The worry with differentiating the curriculum in this way is that the presence of these areas, like a familiar picture on a wall, may go unnoticed, until the space they once inhabited is empty, reminding us of what has been lost.

Yet, writing about creativity and connection in young children Tim Loughton and Sarah Teather, coalition ministers from the Department for Children and Families affirmed the importance of play in early childhood reasoning:

Not only is cognitive development faster in those formative years than at any other time in our lives, and therefore more important to nurture, but scientists have also argued for some time now that play in childhood creates a brain that has greater behavioural flexibility and improved potential for learning later in life thanks to its complex evaluations of playmates, ideas of reciprocity and the use of specific signals and rules. In other words, the creative inputs we receive in the nursery very directly translate into the educational and industrial outputs of tomorrow.

(Loughton and Teather, 2010: 47)

Pragmatic though their reasoning may be play is indeed a necessity in early childhood which should not be compromised – and, since much free play outside of school hours has been eroded for a variety of reasons the time children have for untrammelled exploration is greatly reduced, particularly out of doors. This suggests an additional role for early years education: to provide essential experiences for young children that connect them with the cultural and social world and with the environment.

Indeed as Shirley Brice Heath, an American linguistic anthropologist and Professor Emerita, at Stanford University proposes:

If societies wish young learners (and learners across the lifespan) to be creative, especially in the sciences and arts, the young must have free play to watch, imitate, model, discover and explore in the openness afforded by the outdoor world. Most sciences and all arts rely in one way or another on direct experience, sustained practice and creative reflection around meaning.

(Brice Heath, 2010: 122)

Ironically there is a danger that progress can lead to loss of such things as time to play in early childhood and to a loss of human contact due to technological advances developed to the point where, according to Professor John Kounios *'In the modern world, we are constantly bombarded by emails, text messages, cell phone calls, meetings and the demand to be available 24/7'* (BBC Science, Kounious, 2013), leaving little time for reflection or space for thinking. This suggests that if we are to create a curriculum for the twenty-first century through the revised EYFS the emphasis should be upon supporting children across all areas of development, not valuing one domain, or area of learning above another which would serve to narrow children's education, since in the words of Liz Truss, another government minister discussing childcare *'We are in a challenging global environment where we must use the best of everyone's talents. We need to support our children to be able to succeed in a world that is fast-changing'* (DfE, 2013: 13). How we support children in this fast changing world is clearly a matter of diverse opinion – successful learning is more than memorising information or learning scripts to shape behavioural responses, it is connected with social, ethical and moral development, described as the interface between cognition and emotion from which *'emerge the origins of creativity – the artistic, scientific and technological innovations that are unique to our species'* (Immordino-Yang and Damasio, 2007: 7).

Therefore, as we prepare young children for a future which we ourselves cannot fully conceive of nor anticipate precisely we should take heart that young children are thought by scientists to be *'causal learning machines . . . small human versions of the Mars rovers that roam about getting into things on the red planet – except that children are also mission control, interpreting the data they collect'* (Gopnik, 2004: 27), in other words children's incursions into the world through playing and acting upon it are crucial in developing their intellectual capacities, allowing them *'to learn far more about the world around them than any other animals, and to use that knowledge to change the world'* (Gopnik, 2004: 28). The recent publication of a 'good level of development' by government to measure children's success in the EYFS omits inclusion of Understanding the World and Expressive Arts and Design, to some degree placing these areas of learning in the second division, even though the EYFS proposes that all areas of learning are equally important. If we want a society where culture and creativity survive we should focus our efforts on encouraging children to play, to ponder, to reflect, to engage and to withdraw and to be creative whether they are creative mathematicians, furniture designers or scientists. As science is beginning to reveal, it may be the very areas we are relegating to the second division that may be just what we need in the future – to develop an Understanding of the World children need to know about the past and to understand why and how places and communities developed: the basis of concepts of change and cause and effect and inferential understanding – and, through being imaginative and exploring materials children learn about uncertainty and how they can use the same materials in different ways. Creativity and connectedness may be our touchstones for the future – these develop when children learn that they are important. The danger is that children may learn they are unimportant. A world where we are indifferent to creativity and connectedness is not an attractive proposition. Warning against a loss of creativity in anticipation of the publication of the EYFS, Anna Craft, Professor of Education at the University of Exeter and the Open University quotes Jerome Bruner, reminding us that: *'How one conceives of education . . . is a function of how one conceives of culture and its aims, professed and otherwise'* (Craft, 2012: 36). In our haste to ensure children learn the necessary skills such as those discussed throughout this book it will be important to debate which if any are more important. Einstein was no obvious genius at school because he preferred to ponder the sky or problems of his own invention – allowing children time to play leads to children identifying problems which they want to solve: pedagogy in the early years is about bringing children's own ideas to fruition by building on their interests, expanding their 'vision' to see many possibilities and teaching all seven areas in equal proportion.

In the short term the revised EYFS will shape the curriculum, however, the curriculum is ours to create; how we choose to develop it will shape children's lives; how we shape children's lives will the shape the future – and, since *'Childhood and caregiving is fundamental to our humanity'* (Gopnik, 2010: 81) the future of humanity is in all of our hands. Children deserve the best start we can provide – the publication of the revised EYFS should signal the beginning of a new debate about early childhood education so that as this century progresses, and today's young children inherit the world we have created, they will be enabled to shape a future that is in tune with democratic values, and concerned with how best to preserve society and the natural and built environment for future generations. Early education is the launch pad for the *'small human versions of the Mars rovers'* referred to earlier: early childhood is a time for finding a direction, to *'roam about, getting into things on the red planet'* (Gopnik, 2004: 27). Roamers learn, but roaming, like learning can sometimes be difficult to make sense of since learning pathways are not always linear, nor are learning trajectories always immediately measurable. The art is in making young children's learning visible and as advocates of children helping policy makers to understand its value.

References

Abbott, L. and Edminston, B. (2006) *Curriculum and Pedagogy in the Classroom* Available at Mantle of the Expert. Com: http://www.mantleoftheexpert.com/studying/articles/BE%20LA%20-%20 Curriculum%20and%20Pedagogy%20in%20the%20Classroom.pdf [Accessed 7 January 2013].

Ackerman, D. J. and Barnett, W. Steven (2005) *Prepared for Kindergarten: What Does 'Readiness' Mean?* NIEER Policy Brief. New Brunswick, NJ: NIEER. Available at http://nieer.org/resources/policyreports/ report5.pdf [Accessed on 2 April 2013].

Allen, Graham, MP (2011) *Early Intervention: The Next Steps, An Independent Report to Her Majesty's Government.* London: Cabinet Office.

American Academy of Pediatrics (2011) *Media Use by Children Younger than 2 Years Pediatrics*; originally published online October 17, 2011; Council on Communications and Media. Available at http://pediatrics. aappublications.org/content/early/2011/10/12/peds.2011-1753.full.pdf [Accessed 7 April 2013].

Anda, R. F., Butchart, A., Felitti, V. J. and Brown, D. W. (2010) Building a Framework for Global Surveillance of the Public Health Implications of Adverse Childhood Experiences. Reprinted from *American Journal of Preventive Medicine*, Volume 39, No. 1. Available at http://icmhp.org/newsevents/Tues-06-26-12/1/Global%20 Surveillance%20of%20Public%20Health%20ACEs.pdf [Accessed 2 April 2013].

Armbuster, B., Lehr, F. and Osborn, J. (2006) *A Child Becomes a Reader: Proven Ideas from Research for Parents.* Portsmouth, New Hampshire: National Institute for Literacy.

Auld, Shelley (2002) Five Key Principles of Heuristic Play. *New Zealand Journal of Infant and Toddler Education*, Volume 4, No. 2. Available at: http://www.lead.ece.govt.nz/~/media/Educate/Files/Reference%20 Downloads/infants%20toddlerissue3.pdf [Accessed 2 January 2013].

Australian Government Department of Education, Employment and Workplace Relations for the Council of Australian Governments (2010) *Educators: Belonging, Being and Becoming: Educators' Guide to the Early Years Learning Framework for Australia.* Available at http://www.ag.gov. au/cca [Accessed December 2012].

Barker, R. (2011) *Report of the Inquiry into Overcoming Barriers to Literacy*: All-Party Parliamentary Group for Education.

Baum, Dr N., Bamberger, E., M.A. and Anchor, Dr Chava (2005) *Building Resilience in Preschool Children: A Preschool Teachers' Manual*. Jerusalem: The Temmy and Albert Latner Center. Available at http://bernardvanleer. org/files/ICTP_Preschool_Resilience_Manual_English.pdf [Accessed 3 April 2013].

Berninger, V. and Amtmann, D. (2003) Preventing written expression disabilities through early and continuing assessment and intervention for handwriting and/or spelling problems: Research into Practice. In H. Swanson, K. Harris and S. Graham (eds) *Handbook of Learning Disabilities*. New York: The Guilford Press.

Brice Heath, S. (2010) Born Creative: Play in nature: The foundation of creative thinking. In Tims, C. (ed.) *Creative learning in the early years is not just child's play . . . Born Creative*. Collection 29 DEMOS. Available at www.demos.co.uk [Accessed 7 April 2013].

Britto, Pia Rebello, Ph.D (Updated April 2012) *School Readiness: A Conceptual Framework*. United Nations Children's Fund, New York: Available at http://www.unicef.org/education/files/Chil2Child_Conceptual Framework_FINAL(1).pdf [Accessed on 30 March 2013].

Brotherson, S. (2009) *Supporting Physical Growth and Development in Young Children*. Fargo, Dakota 58105: NDSU Extension Service.

Brouillette, L. (2010) How the Arts Help Children to Create Healthy Social Scripts: Exploring the Perceptions of Elementary Teachers. *Arts Education Policy Review*, 111: 16–24. Heldref Publications. Available at http://gse. uci.edu/docs/Arts_Policy_social_emotional_development.pdf [Accessed 7 April 2013].

Buckley, B. (2003) *Children's Communication Skills From Birth to Five Years*. Oxford: Routledge, Taylor & Francis Group.

California Department of Education (2010) *California Pre-school Curriculum Framework*. Sacramento, California.

Californian Preschool Instruction Network (CPIN) (2006) *Developmental Writing* Presentation. Available at http://www.cpin.us/docs/mod_ writing2.3.06final.pdf [Accessed 6 April 2013].

Carle, E. (1988) *The Mixed-Up Chameleon*. Harmondsworth: Puffin Books.

Centre on the Developing Child: Harvard University (2011) *Building the Brain's 'Air Traffic Control' System*: How Early Experiences Shape the Development of Executive Function Working Paper 11.

Chard, D.J. and Dickson, S.V. (undated) *Phonological Awareness: Instructional and Assessment Guidelines*. Available at http://www.readingrockets.org/ article/6254/ [Accessed 19 February 2013].

Chawla, L. (2012) The Importance of Access to Nature for Young Children. In *Living Conditions: The Influence on Young Children's Health. Early Childhood Matters.* June: 118. The Hague: Bernard van leer Foundation.

Cole, J. (1997) *I'm a Big Sister.* New York: Harper Collins Publishers.

Cole, J. (1997) *I'm a Big Brother.* New York: Harper Collins Publishers.

Committee for Economic Development (CED) (2012) A Statement by the Policy and Impact Committee of the Committee for Economic Development. In *Unfinished Business: Continued Investment in Child Care and Early Education is Critical to Business and America's Future.* Available at http://www.ncsl.org/documents/cyf/CEDUnfinished BusinessReportpdf.pdf [Accessed 1 April 2013].

Communication Trust (2010) *All Together Now Toolkit.* Available at http://www.thecommunicationtrust.org.uk/resources/resources/hello-campaign-resources/all-together-now.aspx [Accessed 5 April 2013].

Council for the Curriculum, Examinations and Assessment (CCEA) (2006) *Developing Fundamental Movement Skills: Teacher's Guide, Foundation Stage: Physical Development.* Available at www.ccea.org.uk, Belfast [Accessed January 2013].

Council for the Curriculum, Examinations and Assessment (CCEA) (2006) *Language and Literacy in the Foundation Stage: Reading.* Northern Ireland Curriculum Early Years Literacy Group Available at http://www.nicurriculum.org.uk/docs/foundation_stage/areas_of_learning/language_and_literacy/LL_Reading.pdf [Accessed 6 April 2013].

Craft, A. (2012) Born Creative: Deconstruction or reconstruction? New directions in policies for creativity in the early years. DEMOS. In Tims, C. (ed.) *Creative learning in the early years is not just child's play . . . Born Creative.* Collection 29 DEMOS. Available at www.demos.co.uk [Accessed 7 April 2013].

Crawford, C., Dearden, L. and Greaves, E. (2011) *Does When You Are Born Matter? The impact of month of birth on children's cognitive and non-cognitive skills in England.* A Report to the Nuffield Foundation (Institute of Fiscal Studies). Available at http://www.ifs.org.uk/bns/bn122.pdf [Accessed on 2 April 2013].

Cremin, T., Barnard, P. and Craft, A. (2006) *Pedagogy and Possibility Thinking in the Early Years. Thinking Skills and Creativity.* Available at http://oro.open.ac.uk/6544/1/6544.pdf [Accessed 4 April 2013].

Cross, C.T., Woods, T. A. and Schweingruber, H. (Eds) (2009) *Mathematics Learning in: Paths Towards Excellence and Equity Early Childhood.* Committee on Early Childhood Mathematics; National Research Council.

Cross, K. Patricia (1999) Learning is About Making Connections. *The Cross Papers* No. 3, League for Innovation in the Community College. Available at http://www.djames84.net/Cert_51/Learning%20Is%20About%20Connections.pdf [Accessed 22 January 2013].

Cryer, D., Harms, T. and Riley, C. (2004) *All About the ITERS-R*. Lewisville, NC: Kaplan Early Learning Company.

Dale McManis, L. and Gunnewig, S. B. (2012) Finding the Education in Educational Technology with Early Learners, *Young Children*, May 2012, National Association for the Education of Young Children (NAEYC).

Delany, K. (2011). *Waking the 'Third Teacher': the Whys and Hows. Te Whāriki; Principle to Practice.* Available at http://elp.co.nz/ EducationalLeadershipProject_Resources_Articles_ELP.php [Accessed December 2012].

Department for Children, Schools and Families (DCSF) (2008a) *Letters and Sounds: Principles and Practice of High Quality Phonics Phase One Teaching Programme.* Crown Copyright.

Department for Children, Schools and Families (DCSF) (2008b) *The Impact of Parental Involvement on Children's Education.* Annesley, Nottingham: DCSF Publications.

Department for Children, Schools and Families (DCSF) (2009a) *Children Thinking Mathematically: PSRN.* Annersley, Nottingham: DCSF Publications.

Department for Children, Schools and Families (DCSF) (2009b) *Numbers and Patterns: Laying Foundations in Mathematics.* The National Strategies: Primary.

Department for Education, (DfE) (2011) *Reforming the Early Years Foundation Stage (the EYFS): Government Response to Consultation.* Available at https://www.education.gov.uk/publications/eOrdering Download/DFE-00298-2011.pdf [Accessed on 1 April 2013].

Department for Education (DfE) (2012) *Statutory Framework for the Early Years Foundation Stage.* Available at https://www.education.gov. uk/publications/standard/AllPublications/Page1/DFE-00023-2012 [Accessed 28 March 2013].

Department for Education (DfE) (2012a) *What is the research evidence on writing?* Education Standards Research Team, Department for Education.

Department for Education (DfE) (2013) *More Great Childcare Report: Raising quality and giving parents more choice.* January. Available at https://www.education.gov.uk/publications/eOrderingDownload/ More%20Great%20Childcare%20v2.pdf [Accessed 7 April 2013].

Department for Education (DfE) and Department of Health (DoH) (2011) *Supporting Families in the Foundation Years.* Available at http://media. education.gov.uk/assets/files/pdf/s/supporting%20families%20in%20 the%20foundation%20years.pdf [Accessed 3 April 2013].

Department for Education and Skills (DfES) (2003) *Birth to Three Matters.* London: DfES/Sure Start.

Department for Education and Skills (DfES) (2007) *Statutory Framework for the Early Years Foundation Stage Setting the Standards for Learning, Development and Care for Children from Birth to Five.* Annesley Nottingham: DFES publications.

Department for Education/Early Education (DfE/EE) (2012) *Development Matters in the Early Years Foundation Stage* (EYFS). Available at: https://www.education.gov.uk/publications/ContentImages/ProductThumbnails/DEVELOPMENT-MATTERS.gif [Accessed on 28 March 2013].

Department for Education, Statistical First Release (DfE/SFR) (2012) (SFR 13/2012) *Provision For Children Under Five Years Of Age In England.* January. Available at http://www.education.gov.uk/rsgateway/DB/SFR/s001074/sfr13-2012.pdf [Accessed 2 April 2013].

Department for Education, Statistical First Release (DfE/SFR) (SFR 23/2012) *Early Years Foundation Stage Profile Results In England, 2011/12 (17 October 2012).* Available at http://www.education.gov.uk/rsgateway/DB/SFR/ [Accessed 6 April 2013]. DfE (2012).

Department of Health (DoH) (2012) *National Child Measurement Programme: England, 2011/12 school year December 2012.* The Health and Social Care Information Centre. Available at https://catalogue.ic.nhs.uk/publications/public-health/obesity/nati-chil-meas-prog-eng-2011-2012/nati-chil-meas-prog-eng-2011-2012-rep.pdf [Accessed 5 April 2013].

Dewey, J. (ed.: Alfred L. Hall-Quest) (undated) *Experience and Education.* Kappa Delta Pi Publications. Available at http://ruby.fgcu.edu/courses/ndemers/colloquium/experienceducationdewey.pdf [Accessed 5 April 2013].

Diamond, A. (2010) The Evidence Base for Improving School Outcomes by Addressing the Whole Child and by Addressing Skills and Attitudes, Not Just Content. *Early Education and Development,* Volume 21 (5): 780–793. Oxford: Taylor & Francis Group.

Donaldson, J. (2010) *What the Ladybird Heard.* London: Macmillan Children's Books.

Donaldson, M. (1978) *Children's Minds,* London: Harper Collins, Fontana Press.

Duffy, B. (2010) Using creativity and creative learning to enrich the lives of young children at the Thomas Coram Centre. In Tims, C. (ed.) *Creative learning in the early years is not just child's play . . . Born Creative.* Collection 29 DEMOS. Available at www.demos.co.uk [Accessed 7 April 2013].

Education, Audiovisual and Culture Executive Agency (EACEA) (2009) *Tackling Social and Cultural Inequalities through Early Childhood Education and Care in Europe.* Brussels: Eurydice. Available at http://

eacea.ec.europa.eu/about/eurydice/documents/098EN.pdf [Accessed 2 April 2013].

Education Department of Western Australia (1997) *Writing Developmental Continuum*. Sydney: Rigby-Heinemann.

Elkind, D. (2012) *The Many Modes of Experience and Learning: The Grandmasters of ECE*. Exchange Press. Available at https://ccie-catalog. s3.amazonaws.com/library/5020308.pdf [Accessed 23 January 2013].

Evangleou, M., Sylva, K., Edwards, A. and Smith, T. (2008) *Supporting Parents in Promoting Early Learning: The Evaluation of the Early Learning Partnership Project*. Department for Children School and Families. Research Report DCSF RR039.

Feigenson, L., Carey. S. and Hauser, M. (2002) The Representations Underlying Infants' Choice of More: Object File Versus Analog Magnitudes. *Psychological Science*, Volume 13, No 2. March. American Psychological Society.

Field, Frank (2010) *The Foundation Years: Preventing Poor Children Becoming Poor Adults*. The report of the Independent Review on Poverty and Life Chances. London: Cabinet Office.

Gerhardt, S. (2004) *Why Love Matters: How Affection Shapes a Baby's Brain*. East Sussex: Brunner-Routledge, Taylor & Francis Group.

Glover, J. (2009) *Bouncing Back: How can resilience be promoted in vulnerable children and young people?* Barnardo's. Available at http://www.barnardos. org.uk/bouncing_back_resilience_march09.pdf [Accessed 3 April 2013].

Goodall, J. and Vorhaus, J. with the help of Jon Carpentieri, Greg Brooks, Rodie Akerman and Alma Harris (2011) *Review of Best Practice in Parental Engagement* DfE/Institute of Education DfE Research Report DFE-RR156. Available at http://review%20of%20best%20practice%20 in%20parental%20engagement%20dfe/Institute%20of%20Education [Accessed 3 April 2013].

Gopnik, A. (2004) *Finding Our Inner Scientist*. Available at http://www. amacad.org/publications/winter2004/gopnik.pdf [Accessed 7 April 2013].

Gopnik, A. (2009) Your Baby Is Smarter Than You Think. *New York Times*. Available at http://www.nytimes.com/2009/08/16/opinion/16gopnik. html?pagewanted=all&_r=0 [Accessed 6 January 2013]

Gopnik, A. (2010) How Babies Think. *Scientific American*. Available at www. ScientificAmerican.com July 2010. [Accessed 7 April 2013].

Greenaway, R. (undated) *Active Reviewing Guide*. Available at Experiential learning articles + critiques of David Kolb's theory http:// reviewing.co.uk/research/experiential.learning.htm#26#ixzz2IngrSDvi [Accessed 23 January 2013].

Hartshorne, M. (reprinted 2009) I CAN Talk: The Cost to the Nation of Children's Poor Communication Issue 2, London: National Children's Bureau.

Henderson, K. (1999) *The Baby Dances*. London: Walker Books Ltd.

High, P. and the Committee on Early Childhood, Adoption, and Dependent Care and Council on School Health (2008) *School Readiness*. American Academy of Pediatrics. Available at http://pediatrics.aappublications. org/content/121/4/e1008.full.html [Accessed 1 April 2013].

Hughes, B. (2005) Keynote Speech to US/UK Early Years Conference *Building the Case for Economic Investments in Preschool*. Convened by the Partnership for America's Economic Success, with support from the Committee for Economic Development and PNC Financial Services, Inc. Tuesday, January 10, 2006. Available at http://www.readynation. org/docs/2006conference/trans_2006earlyedconf_hughes.pdf [Accessed December 2012].

Hughes, S. (2002) *Dogger*, London: Random House Children's Books.

Hunt, Dr S., Virgo, Dr S., Klett-Davies, Dr M., Page, A. and Apps, J. (2011) *Provider Influence on the Early Home Learning Environment (EHLE)* Department for Education Research Report DFE- RR142. Available at https://www.education.gov.uk/publications/eOrderingDownload/ DFE-RR142.pdf [Accessed 3 April 2013].

I CAN (2008) Fact Sheet Support for Professionals: *Language Difficulties in the Early Years*. London: I CAN. www.talkingpoint.org.uk

I CAN (2011) Primary Milestones Poster: *What's Typical Talk at Primary?* www.talkingpoint.org.uk

Immordino-Yang, M.H. and Damasio, A. (2007) We Feel, Therefore We Learn: The Relevance of Affective and Social Neuroscience to Education. *International Journal Mind, Brain and Education*, Volume 1, Oxford: Blackwell Publishing Inc. Available at http://olms.cte.jhu.edu/olms/ data/resource/8038/Week%204_Article%20We%20Feel%20 Therefore%20We%20Learn.pdf [Accessed 7 April 2013].

Institute of Medicine (IOM) and National Research Council (NRC) (2012) *From Neurons to Neighbourhoods: An Update*: Workshop Summary. Washington, DC: The National Academies Press.

Jasmin, K. (2012) *Testimony prepared for the NY Education Reform Commission Public Hearing*, Bank Street College, New York on 16th October 2012. Available at http://www.governor.ny.gov/assets/documents/101612_ NYCHearing/KimJasminTestimony.pdf [Accessed 2 April 2013].

Kellmer Pringle, Mia (1980) *The Needs of Children*. London: Hutchinson.

Kelly, Y., Sacker, A. and Del Bono, E. *et al.* (2011) *What role for the home learning environment and parenting in reducing the socioeconomic gradient in child development? Findings from the Millenium Cohort Study*. Available at http://www.bookstart.org.uk/usr/library/documents/main/kelly-mcs-study.pdf [Accessed 3 April 2013].

Kernan, M. (2012) *Parental Involvement in Early Learning: A Review of Research, Policy and Practice*. The Hague: International Child

Development Initiatives (ICDI) Leiden on behalf of Bernard van Leer Foundation.

Laevers, F. (2011 online publication) Experiential Education: Making Care and Education More Effective Through Well-Being and Involvement. In *Encyclopedia on Early Childhood Development*. Accessed at http://www. child-encyclopedia.com/documents/LaeversANGxp1.pdf

Langston, A. and Doherty, J. (2012) *The Revised EYFS in Practice: Thinking, Reflecting and Doing*. London: Bloomsbury/Featherstone Press.

Lascano, R. E. (2004) *The Link Between Philosophy for Children and Resilience*. The Hague: Early Childhood Matters, Bernard Van Leer Foundation. Available at http://www.bernardvanleer.org/Critical_thinking?pubnr= 531&download=1 [Accessed 3 April 2013].

Lave, J. and Wenger, E. (1991) *Situated Learning: Legitimate Peripheral Participation*. Cambridge: Cambridge University Press.

Lockhart, S. (2012) *High Scope Extensions*. Volume 26, No. 3: 11. High Scope Press.

Lonigan, C. J. and Shanahan, T. (2008) Executive Summary of the Report of the National Panel: A Scientific Synthesis of Early Literacy Development and Implications for Intervention. In National Early Literacy Panel Report: *Developing Early Literacy. Report to the National Early Literacy Panel*. Available at http://www.nifl.gov [Accessed February 2013].

Loughton, T. and Teather, S. (2010) Creating conditions: Trusted professional and targeted resources for creativity in the early years. In Tims, C. (ed.) *Creative learning in the early years is not just child's play . . . Born Creative*. Collection 29 DEMOS. Available at www.demos.co.uk [Accessed 7 April 2013].

Maslow, Abraham. (1987) *Motivation and Personality, Third Edition*. New York: Harper.

Masten, A. S. and Gerwitz, A. H. (2006) Resilience in Development: The Importance of Early Childhood. In Tremblay, R.E., Barr, R.G. and Peters, R.D. (eds) *Encyclopedia on Early Childhood Development*. 2006:1– 6 Available at: http://www.child-encyclopedia.com/documents/Masten-GewirtzANGxp.pdf [Accessed 25 October 2012].

McCain, M.N., Mustard, J.F. and McCuaig, K. (2011) *Early Years Study 3: Making Decisions, Taking Action*. Toronto: Margaret & Wallace McCain Family Foundation.

McKee, D. (1989) *Elmer the Elephant*. London: Anderson Press Ltd.

McMahon Giles, R. and Wellhousen Tucks, K. (2010) Children Write Their World: Environmental print as a Teaching Tool. In *Dimensions of Early Childhood*, Volume 38, No. 3. Fall. Available from http://www. SouthernEarlyChildhood.org

Meiners. J. (2008) *The Arts in the Early Years Learning Framework*. National Advocates for Arts Education, School of Education, South Australia.

Michael Cohen Group LLC (2011) *Young Children, Apps and iPads*. Research undertaken as part of the evaluation activities of the U.S. Department of Education Ready to Learn Program prepared by Michael Cohen Group LLC, New York. Available at http://mcgrc.com/wp-content/uploads/2012/06/ipad-study-cover-page-report-mcg-info_new-online.pdf [Accessed 7 April 2013].

Miller, E. and Almon, J. (2009) *Crisis in the Kindergarten: Why Children Need to Play in School*. College Park, MD: Alliance for Childhood, 2009.

Miller, S. (2008) *Secure Attachment*, Chicago: Ounce of Prevention Fund. Available at http://www.ounceofprevention.org/research/pdfs/SecureAttachment.pdf [Accessed 2 April 2013].

Moyles, J., Adams, S. and Musgrove, A. (2002) *SPEEL Study of Pedagogical Effectiveness in Early Learning*, DfE Research Report 363.

Murphy, J. (2007) *Whatever Next?* London: Macmillan Children's Books.

NAEYC (2012) *Technology and Interactive Media as Tools in Early Childhood Programs Serving Children from Birth through Age 8*. Joint position statement of the National Association for the Education of Young Children and the Fred Rogers Center for Early Learning and Children's Media at Saint Vincent College.

National Children's Bureau (NCB) (2012) *A Know How Guide: The EYFS Progress Check at Two*. Online Publication: Department for Education.

National Research Council (NRC) and Institute of Medicine (IOM) (2000) *From Neurons to Neighbourhoods: The Science of Early Childhood Development*. Committee on Integrating the Science of Early Childhood Development. Jack P. Shonkoff and Deborah A. Phillips (eds) Board on Children, Youth and Families, Commission on Behavioural and Social Sciences and Education. Washington DC: National Academies Press.

National Scientific Council on the Developing Child (2004). *Young children develop in an environment of relationships*. Working Paper No. 1. Updated 2009. Available at http://www.developingchild.net [Accessed 23 October 2012].

New Zealand (NZ) Ministry of Education (1996) *Te Whāriki: Early Childhood Curriculum*. Wellington, NZ: Learning Media.

Nutbrown, C. and Hannon, P. (2011) *Environmental Print in Early Literacy Development*. From real-online.group.shef.ac.uk.

OECD (2012) *Research Brief: Parental and Community Engagement Matters*. Available at www.oecd.org/edu/school/49322478.pdf [Accessed 3 April 2013].

OFSTED (2011) *Getting Them Reading Early: Module 3 Principles of high quality phonic work*. Available at http://www.ofsted.gov.uk/resources/getting-them-reading-early [Accessed 6 April 2013].

Pajares, F. and Schunk, DH. (2002) Self And Self-Belief In Psychology and Education: An Historical Perspective. In J. Aronson (ed.) *Improving Academic Achievement*. New York: Academic Press. Available at http://www.uky.edu/~eushe2/Pajares/PSHistoryOfSelf.PDF [Accessed 16 February 2013].

Pascal, C. (2011) *Definitions of Teaching and School Readiness*. Drawn from a dialogue at the Early Education Group. Available at http://www.bishopg.ac.uk/docs/PDE/CPRSchoolReadiness.pdf [Accessed 12 December 2012].

Pen Green (2005) *Pen Green Framework for Engaging Parents*. Corby, England: Pen Green Centre.

Plowman, L. *et al.* (2012) *Young Children Learning with Toys and Technology at Home*. Research Briefing April 2012, No. 8, School of Education, University of Stirling.

Qualifications and Curriculum Authority (QCA) (2000) *Curriculum Guidance for the Foundation Stage*. London: Qualifications and Curriculum Authority. Available at http://www.smartteachers.co.uk/upload/documents_32.pdf [Accessed 4 April 2013].

Queensland Studies Authority (2006) *Early Years Curriculum Guidelines*. Brisbane: The State of Queensland. Website: www.qsa.qld.edu.au.

Raikes, H. H. and Pope Edwards, C. (2009) *Extending the Dance in Infant and Toddler Caregiving*. Baltimore, MA: Paul H. Brookes Publishing Co. Inc.

Rhode Island Kids Count (2005) *Getting Ready: Findings from the National School Readiness Indicators Initiative. A 17 State Partnership*. Sponsored by the David and Lucile Packard Foundation, the Kauffman Foundation and the Ford Foundation. Available at http://www.gettingready.org/matriarch/d.asp?PageID=303&PageName2=pdfhold&p=&PageName=Getting+Ready+%2D+Full+Report%2Epdf [Accessed 2 April 2013].

Riley-Ayers, S. and Barnett, S. (2012) The Role of Early Education in Language and Literacy Development. *Encyclopedia of Language and Literacy Development* (pp. 1–8). London, ON: Canadian Language and Literacy Research Network. Available at http://literacyencyclopedia.ca/pdfs/topic.php?topId+307 [Accessed January 2013].

Ritter, S. M., van Baaren, R. B. and Dijksterhuis, A. (2012) Creativity: The role of unconscious processes in idea generation and idea selection. *Thinking Skills and Creativity*, Volume 7, Issue 1: 21–27 April. Elsevier journal home page: http://www.elsevier.com/locate/tsc

Rose, J. (2006) *Independent Review of the Teaching of Early Reading, Final Report*, March 2006. Annesley, Nottingham: DfES.

Rosen, M. and Oxenbury, H. (1989) *We're Going on a Bear Hunt*. London: Walker Books.

Saskatchewan Ministry of Education, Early Learning and Child Care Branch (2008) *Play and Exploration Early Learning Programme Guide.* Available at http://www.education.gov.sk.ca/Default.aspx?DN=c711842e-23aa-4e82-b33d-4a530f8d4b2f [Accessed 5 April 2013].

Share, M., Kerrins, L. and Greene, S. (2011) *Early Years Professionalism: An Evaluation of the Early Learning Initiative's Professional Development Programme in Community Childcare Centres in the Dublin Docklands.* Dublin: National College of Ireland.

Sharp, C. (2004) *Developing Young Children's Creativity: What Can We Learn from Research?* Paper presented to an Invitational Seminar NFER. Available at https://www.nfer.ac.uk/nfer/publications/55502/55502.pdf [Accessed 7 April 2013].

Sharples, J., Slavin, R., Chambers, B. and Sharp, C. (2011) Effective classroom strategies for closing the gap in educational achievement for children and young people living in poverty, including white working-class boys. *CEO Schools and Communities Research Review* 4. Available at http://www.c4eo.org.uk/themes/schools/classroomstrategies/files/classroom_strategies_research_review.pdf [Accessed 19 February 2013].

Sharratt, N. and Goodhart, P. (2000) *You Choose.* London: Random House Books.

Siegler, R., DeLoache, J. and Eisenberg, N. (2011) *How Children Develop. (Third Edition) International Edition.* New York: Worth Palgrave Macmillan.

Siraj-Blatchford, I. and Siraj-Blatchford, J. (2009) *Improving children's attainment through a better quality of family-based support for early learning.* London: Centre for Excellence and Outcomes in Children and Young People's Services (C4EO).

Siraj-Blatchford, I., Sylva, K., Muttock, S., Gilden, R. and Bell, D. (2002) *Researching Effective Pedagogy in the Early Years.* DfES.

Skoe, E. and Kraus, N. (2012) A Little Goes A Long Way: How the Adult Brain Is Shaped by Musical Training in Early Childhood. *The Journal of Neuroscience*, August 22, 32(34):11507–11510 – 11507. Available at http://www.soc.northwestern.edu/brainvolts/documents/SkoeKraus_JNeurosci_2012.pdf [Accessed 7 April 2013].

Standards and Testing Agency (STA) (2012) *Early Years Foundation Stage Profile Handbook 2013.* Available at www.education.gov.uk/assessment [Accessed 2 April 2013].

Standards and Testing Agency (STA) (2013a) *EYFSP Profile Exemplification*: ELG10: Writing. Available at http://media.education.gov.uk/assets/files/pdf/e/elg10-writing.pdf [Accessed 7 April 2013].

Standards and Testing Agency (STA) (2013b) EYFS Exemplification ELG11: Numbers. Available at http://www.education.gov.uk/schools/teachingandlearning/assessment/eyfs/b00217443/eyfs-exemplification/eyfs-elg-11 [Accessed 7 April 2013].

Sylva, K., Melhuish, E., Sammons, P., Siraj-Blatchford, I. and Taggart, B. (2004) *Effective Preschool Education*, Final Report. DFES, London Institute of Education.

TACTYC (2011) *Occasional Paper 1: The Early Years Foundation Stage Through the Daily Experiences of Children.*

The Communication Trust: Hartshorne, M. with Cross, M. and Burns, M. (2011) *Misunderstood*. London: The Communication Trust

The New York State Dept. (2011/12) *New York State Prekindergarten Foundation for the Common Core*. Albany, New York: The New York State Dept.

Tickell, Dame Clare (2011) *The Early Years: Foundations for life, health and learning*. An Independent Report on the Early Years Foundation Stage to Her Majesty's Government.

Tillman, N. (2005) *On the Night You Were Born*. Tualatin, Oregon: Darling Press.

Twigg, D. and Garvis, S. (2010) Exploring Art in Early Childhood Education. *The International Journal of The Arts in Society*, Volume 5, No. 2, 2010. Available at http://www.arts-journal.com [Accessed 7 April 2013].

United Nations General Assembly (UN) (2002) S-27/2. *A world fit for children Resolution*. Adopted by the General Assembly [*on the report of the Ad Hoc Committee of the Whole (A/S-27/19/Rev.1 and Corr.1 and 2)*]. Available at http://www.unicef.org/specialsession/docs_new/documents/ A-RES-S27-2E.pdf [Accessed on line 1 April 2013]

University of Minnesota Amplatz Children's Hospital (2010) *Developmental Skills for Ages 2 to 3 Years*. Available at http://www.fairview.org/fv/ groups/internet/documents/web_content/developmen_2010 09262104505.pdf [Accessed January 2013].

Waldfogel, J. and Washbrook, E. (2008) *Early Years Policy Paper*. Prepared for the Sutton Trust–Carnegie Summit: Social Mobility and Education Policy. June 1–3, 2008. Available at http://www.bristol.ac.uk/ifssoca/ outputs/waldfogeleyp.pdf [Accessed 2 April 2013].

Warden, C. (2010) Children as Designers of their Own Spaces. In *Wonder: Newsletter of the Nature Action Collaborative For Children (NACC)*, March/April. Exchange Magazine.

Washbrook, E. and Waldfogel, J. (2011) *On Your Marks: Measuring the school readiness of children in low-to-middle income families*. Resolution Foundation. Available at http://www.resolutionfoundation.org/media/ media/downloads/On_your_marks.pdf [Accessed on 2 April 2013].

Washington State Department of Early Learning (2012) *Early Learning and Development Guidelines: Birth through 3rd Grade*. Olympia WA.

Whittington, V. (2012) *Executive Function in the Early Years*; An Everyday Learning Series Title: Volume 10 Number 3, (2012) Early Childhood Australia.

Williams, Sir P. (2008) *Independent Review of Mathematics Teaching in Early Years Settings and Primary Schools*, Final Report. DCSF

Winter, P. (2010) *Engaging Families in the Early Childhood Development Story: Neuroscience and Early Childhood Development: Summary of Selected Literature and Key Messages for Parenting.* Early Childhood Services, Department of Education and Children's Services, South Australia. Available at http://www.mceecdya.edu.au/verve/_resources/ECD_Story-Neuroscience_and_early_childhood_dev.pdf [Accessed 2 April 2013].

Witmer, D. (2011) *Attachment: What Works?* Issue 24, February 2011. www.vanderbilt.edu/csefel. Center on the Social and Emotional Foundations for Early Learning: Vanderbilt Kennedy Center for Research on Human Development.

Wylie, C. (2011) *Competent Children, Competent Learners Forming Adulthood Competent Learners @ 20: Summary of Key Findings.* New Zealand Council for Educational Research.

Websites

Chapter 2

Foundation Years Website Accessed at http://www.foundationyears.org.uk/early-years-foundation-stage-2012/ [2 April 2013].

DfE website Accessed at http://www.education.gov.uk/childrenandyoung people/earlylearningandchildcare/a00191780/core-purpose-of-sure-start-childrens-centres [2 April 2013].

Chapter 4

Family and Parenting Institute website: http://www.familyandparenting.org/our_work/All-Other-Subjects/Early-Home-Learning-Matters/Practitioners-Section/Engaging+parents/Barriers-to-parental-involvement

Chapter 5

ABC (Ken Robinson) http://www.abc.net.au/7.30/content/2009/s2600125.htm

Nursery World (2013) accessed on 11 February 2013 at http://bit.ly/WydNeO

Chapter 6

Learning Knowledge Available at: http://www.learning-knowledge.com/self-theories.html [Accessed 31 December 2012].

MEN Media Available at: http://menmedia.co.uk/manchestereveningnews/news/s/1596333_153-languages-being-spoken-in-manchester-but-census-didnt-show-that-says-language-professor [Accessed 22 December 2012].

Makaton Website: Available at http://www.makaton.org/aboutMakaton/howMakatonWorks/ [Accessed 5 April 2013].

Chapter 7

Mantel of the Expert Available at http://www.mantleoftheexpert.com/ [Accessed 7 January 2013].

Chapter 8

CPIN (2006) *Developmental Writing* Presentation Available at http://www.cpin.us/docs/mod_writing2.3.06final.pdf [Accessed 6 April 2013].

Encarta Dictionary (North America). Accessed online.

DfE website SPLD resources (2012): Module: *Specific learning Difficulties Unit 12 Learning to Write* PDF Available at http://www.education.gov.uk/lamb/resources/SpLD/Unit%20PDFs/12_learning_to_write.pdf [Accessed 6 April 2013].

Read, Write Inc. Oxford University Press downloaded at http://www.oxfordschoolimprovement.co.uk/resources/view/rwi-phonics

Chapter 12

BBC Science. Available at http://www.bbc.co.uk/science/0/21660191 [Accessed 16 March 2013].

Big Think. Available at http://bigthink.com/users/kayredfieldjamison [Accessed 16 March 2013].

Index

mathematics 145
personal, social and emotional
development 117
school readiness 18–19, 23
understanding the world 154, 157,
158–61

Visits/visitors 57, 156
Vocabulary 29, 66, 74, 103
mathematics-related 141, 143, 144, 146,
149, 151

Websites 200–1
Well-being 3
World (the)
aspect of understanding the world 155–7,
158–61
see also Understanding the world
Writing 125, 133–9

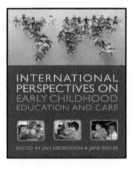

International Perspectives on Early Childhood Education and Care

Jan Georgeson and Jane Payler

9780335245918 (Paperback)
February 2013

eBook also available

There is a growing interest in understanding how early years care and education is organised and experienced internationally. This book examines key influential approaches to early years care as well as some less well-known systems from around the world.

Key features:

- Informs those studying early years about perspectives in other countries
- Encourages critical thinking about issues, influences and the complexities of early years provision around the world
- Promotes critical reflection on students' own provision and the current context of that provision

www.openup.co.uk

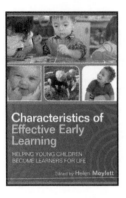

**CHARACTERISTICS OF EFFECTIVE
EARLY LEARNING**
Helping young children become learners
for life

Helen Moylett

9780335263264 (Paperback)
October 2013

eBook also available

The key argument of The Characteristics of Effective Early Learning
is that how children learn is as important as what they learn.
This book helps you understand how to support the learning and
development of young children through promoting the characteristics
of effective early learning: play and exploring, active learning, and
creating and thinking critically.

Key features:

- Investigates how children engage in learning through playing and
  exploring, and are motivated through active learning
- Explores how children become creative and critical thinkers able
  to review their own learning and thinking, imaginatively solving
  problems and excited by their own
- Examines appropriate approaches to observation, assessment
  and planning

www.openup.co.uk

RETHINKING SUPERHERO AND WEAPON PLAY
Superheroes and Children's Moral Development

Steven Popper

9780335247066 (Paperback)
April 2013

eBook also available

This book explores children's war, weapon and superhero play with a view to examining its potential (positive) impact on developing moral values and sensibilities, and to the many moral themes available for children's exploration during their engagement with such play, and the traditional and continuing need for children to receive a good moral education, with reference to many ideas from educational philosophy.

Key features:

- It links examples of children's real-life play and perspectives to theories about play, moral development and narrative psychology
- It explores the continuing attraction of classical dualism (i.e. good versus evil) for children and various educational perspectives about this
- Contains a wealth of learning opportunities and suggestions of ways to use superheroes to advance children's moral, philosophical and emotional thinking

www.openup.co.uk

A–Z OF PLAY IN EARLY CHILDHOOD

Janet Moyles

9780335246380 (Paperback)
2012

eBook also available

This indispensable guide uses a unique glossary format to explore some of the key themes in play in early childhood, many of which regularly arise for students, tutors, parents and practitioners. As well as covering key concepts, theories and influential figures in the field, the book considers important aspects of each construct and highlights the complexity of play in early childhood.

Key features:

- Split into a comprehensive glossary running through elements of play from A–Z, it is a useful, fun and unique companion to understanding children's play
- Original thoughts from well known early years people including Tricia David, Carol Aubrey, Angela Anning and Lilian Katz

www.openup.co.uk